We heared them holler and holler till they couldn't holler no mo! Then they jes' sorta grunt every lick till they die. We finds big streams of blood where he has whooped them.

And when it rained the whole top of the ground jes' looks like a river of blood dere.

—LOU WILLIAMS

FORMER SLAVE QUARTERS, ORMOND PLANTATION,
ST. CHARLES PARISH, LOUISIANA, 1934.
RICHARD KOCH PHOTO

SEVENTY-FIVE
YEARS AFTER THE
CIVIL WAR, THE
LAST VESTIGES OF
SLAVERY IN THE
UNITED STATES WERE
DOCUMENTED.
THE REMAINS OF
PLANTATIONS,
SLAVE QUARTERS,
CABINS AND
BARNS—SOME LONG
ABANDONED—WERE
PHOTOGRAPHED.

**THOUSANDS OF
FORMERLY ENSLAVED
AFRICAN AMERICAN
MEN AND WOMEN
PROVIDED FIRST-
HAND ACCOUNTS OF
LIFE UNDER SLAVERY.**

FORMER SLAVE QUARTERS, DOUGHOREGAN
MANOR, ELLICOTT CITY, MARYLAND, 1936.
E.H. PICKERING PHOTO

NOW, THESE WORDS
AND PICTURES ARE
PAIRED TO OFFER
INSIGHT INTO A
SHAMEFUL TIME IN
AMERICAN HISTORY
THAT RESONATES
TODAY.

RIVER OF BLOOD

PHARR PLANTATION HOUSE, GEORGIA, 1937.
DOROTHEA LANGE PHOTO

AMERICAN SLAVERY FROM THE PEOPLE WHO LIVED IT

Interviews & Photographs of Formerly Enslaved African Americans

Edited by
Richard Cahan and
Michael Williams

Foreword by
Adam Green

This book is funded by a generous grant from:

JONATHAN LOGAN
FAMILY FOUNDATION

Published by CityFiles Press, Chicago, Illinois

Produced and designed by Michael Williams

ISBN: 9780991541850

First Edition

Printed in China

Front cover: Richard Toler, 1937. *Ruth Thompson photo*
Back cover: Lizzie Hill, 1937. *Gertha Couric and Demps B. Oden photo*
Endsheets: Old cable ferry between Camden and Gee's Bend, Alabama, 1939. *Marion Post Wolcott photo*
Page 1: Detail from Marion Post Wolcott photo of cable ferry, Gee's Bend, Alabama, 1939. *Marion Post Wolcott photo*

THE FORKS OF CYPRESS PLANTATION
IN LAUDERDALE COUNTY, ALABAMA.
JAMES JACKSON PHOTO

CONTENTS

RUINS OF THE ELMS PLANTATION,
OTRANTO, SOUTH CAROLINA, 1940.
C.O. GREENE PHOTO

FOREWORD

To be an enslaved African American was to be denied control of body and soul, to be denied rights to protect family, advance personal welfare (to say nothing of prosperity) or pursue better futures. It disregarded, legally and literally, the personhood of those enslaved. As such, American chattel slavery was a brutal and inhuman crime, ranking among the worst committed. It robbed people of their fair share of human being; of spouses, kin, skin, limbs and lives. Racial slavery imposed social and moral hazard in its time—capped by the most devastating war America had or would suffer. It extracts social and moral cost from us still today, toxically fogging hearts and minds, gambling away the precious experiment of democracy itself.

Yet, in the face of abuses and costs, one cannot regard enslaved African Americans, debased and assaulted though they were, as having been *negated*. Subject to exploitation and destruction of family ties, laid bare by law's refusal to respect their sanctity as persons, African Americans who suffered slavery lived, loved, mastered crafts, conspired to run away, resist and revolt. The denial of their *volition*, devastating though it was, could not destroy their *will*. Leveraging this most profound of survivals, later generations of African Americans built a majestic faith, a lustrous culture and a mighty politics. They would, in time, rock the foundations of power and, like the poet Langston Hughes, dream a better America. Better than had ever been imagined. Better than this nation and its history, if truth be told, ever deserved.

We would not know the truths of slavery, or the courage and dignity of those who endured it, had its impact and injuries, its powers *and* limits, not been passed forward to posterity. Flush with indignation and guilt, whites who depended upon and upheld that system could not recognize, much less share, its truths. It was left to African Americans who suffered and survived slavery to name its sins and total its costs while balancing the ledger to leave room for their own worth and capacity as human beings.

This was a tradition that went back to the slave narratives, and the power of first-hand testimony of the enslaved/liberated to quicken the abolition of racial bondage. For generations following Emancipation, it was the living memory of those formerly enslaved that offered new chances to touch America's troubled roots. The most comprehensive pursuit of this fugitive witness, without question, was the vexed and compromised, yet revelatory testimony summoned through the Slave Narrative Collection of the Federal Writers' Project from the 1930s.

The Slave Narrative Collection, recollections of formerly enslaved African Americans through in-person interviews, was, at first glance, a fragile thread through which to weave public understanding of slavery in America.

Whether long or short, each interview was structured around a template of standard questions: birthdate, parents names, type of work, extent of provisions, marriage, family, impressions of freedom following Emancipation and so forth. These required the formerly enslaved to respond to preset inquiries, and likely meant that their notions of life passage and meaning were, too often, left unconsulted. Interviewers, the majority of whom were white, brought biases from that time—not a few of which persist today—regarding their black correspondents' trustworthiness, intelligence and self-respect.

But even under such imperfect conditions, a definitive archive of group memory and appraisal—of selves, of society—was gathered. Over 3,500 individual accounts of lives under slavery and in freedom were eventually archived, from every state of the Confederacy and branching out to many more in the Union. Photographs were taken of more than three hundred of these formally enslaved persons. It is the selection of approximately one hundred of these, together with excerpts from their interviews, that comprises the content of this book, reaffirming the indispensable value of enslaved witnesses to inform the meaning of nation and the power of will.

These encounters with the Slave Narrative Collection were visual, as well as textual, providing richer narratives to interviewers not always prepared to receive them. The arrangement of Sunday suits and dresses in some photographs, the background of implements of trade or craft, the inclusion of portraits of loved ones: these each alluded to life priorities African Americans carried forward from slavery, ones they built out as the bedrock of their freedom.

More indelibly, the trained *gaze* of black men and women, as they recalled exploitation and struggles to get free, compelled respect from their off-frame interviewers, and similarly from the contemporary reader. It is worth noting the advanced, even ancestral age of so many of those interviewed. Having in such cases doubled the average life span of African Americans born *after* slavery's end, they doubtless presumed a measure of respect for that reason, even if others might not be sufficiently acknowledged.

THE PORTRAIT PAINTED OF ENSLAVEMENT was, not surprisingly, devastating. How could it be otherwise, given the grinding regime of labor imposed even on children just weaned? Or the sexual exploitation, whether through assault or compulsion, of enslaved women? Or the separation of families, compelled most often by the cold quest to retire debts and recover liquidity rather than consideration for feelings among the enslaved or on the part of the master? Or the daily brutality, the details of which conform from account to account sufficiently to refute any disbelief, and betray that when whites *did* give voice to feeling, foremost was a burning indignation that their presumed benevolence as masters had not been properly acknowledged?

The myth that slavery was a gentle and necessary school for uncivilized bondsmen and women was disproven through the compilation of these recollections. Generations of historians who would mine them for insight would write a formidable brief that affirmed this truth, first told by the formerly enslaved.

Several interesting anomalies can be discerned within the testimonies. Although

America in the 1930s had undergone massive waves of black migration from the South to the North, raising up black metropolises in New York, Detroit, Chicago and other cities, relatively few of the formerly enslaved themselves chose to relocate to northern communities. No doubt there are practical explanations for this imbalance. Aged out of shifting to an industrial labor pattern, unswayed by the tall tales of nightclubs and street life, and well versed in the conditions of the life they had lived for decades, these individuals offer a valuable witness of what drew many African Americans to southern life, even as their children and grandchildren contemplated the prospects for different lives "up North."

Another striking imbalance can be found in the geographic concentration of these accounts. Nearly two-thirds came from individuals living in Texas. Some of this may be attributed to the resourcefulness and even conscientiousness of those compiling the interviews. Sheldon F. Gauthier, an assistant director at the Fort Worth office of the Works Progress Administration, was credited with taking seventeen of the pictures included here, more than any other photographer. The reason Texas was overrepresented, certainly, was not its example of racial liberalism. During Reconstruction, the state had perhaps the worst record of racial violence. Segregation was instituted as fully there as in Mississippi, Georgia or Alabama. The revived Ku Klux Klan counted Dallas as one of its centers of power in the 1920s.

And yet, formerly enslaved African Americans in Texas who spoke to interviewers introduced a counter narrative to the familiar story of racial supremacy. Many of those living in Texas had originally been born in other slave states. Some had been brought by their parents. Other had chosen to relocate through the search for work or marriage. Those living in East Texas simultaneously navigated the oppression of the cotton belt, while also drawing on the burgeoning freedom heritage of nearby Houston and Galveston, with its Emancipation Park, black cowboys and Juneteenth. The will of those formerly enslaved was to enlarge their freedom and chose their futures. Indeed, movement *within* the South was always as important a source of historical ferment for black folk as movement *from* the South. This is a collateral, yet no less valuable, takeaway from these interviews, read together.

Within a nation obsessed with looking ahead, while averting any searching view of the past, the question of who counts as an ancestor is often left unaddressed, or answered reflexively by caricatured invocation of outsized, deified founders.

The formerly enslaved who lived to tell the story of their bondage and their freedom offer, by comparison, more grounded, less contrived and recognizably human accounts of what it meant to assert a place in this country, as blacks and as Americans. By consulting their claim to person and their witness to the truth, we honor their own life paths and, perhaps, better dignify our own troubled and uncertain journey ahead.

Adam Green is a history professor at the University of Chicago and author of *Selling the Race: Culture and Community in Black Chicago, 1940-1955.* He draws inspiration from his father, Ernest Green, a southerner and a member of the Little Rock Nine.

OLD PLANTATION BELL,
GREENE COUNTY, GEORGIA, 1937.
DOROTHEA LANGE PHOTO

RIVER OF BLOOD

———

Hannah Irwin welcomed the caller into her one-room Alabama home on a high knoll overlooking the winding Chewalla Creek in Eufaula. In Houston, Texas, Sarah Ford put coffee on the fire as she ushered her guest into her cottage. And Walter Calloway sat in the sunshine on his front porch off Avenue F in Birmingham, Alabama.

It was the late 1930s, seven decades after the Emancipation Proclamation. Each of the three elders was getting ready for an interview by writers who came to document their recollections of slavery. The writers, who worked for the Depression-era Works Progress Administration, were compiling the Slave Narrative Collection, an unprecedented endeavor to gather first-hand testimony about one of the darkest chapters of American history. The writers knew that time was running out.

The formerly enslaved, referred to as "informants" by the writers, had lived their young lives in bondage and servitude. Since the Civil War, they had endured the crushing false optimism of Reconstruction and the brutality of Jim Crow. Many had confronted the Ku Klux Klan, fought for the right to vote and suffered through decades of discrimination and injustice. Most lived in extreme poverty.

It took courage to talk.

Stepney Underwood shivered and shook and stuttered, making him difficult to understand. Susan Merritt demurred: "I couldn't tell you how I was treated," she said. But then she recalled in vivid detail the day she was nearly beaten to death.

Most spoke with candor and honesty.

Mary Armstrong called one of her slaveholders "Old Satan." Fannie Moore called hers "a rip-jack." And Richard Toler revealed that the owner of his plantation whipped three or four enslaved people to death.

As their words testify, the former slaves were proud.

"I don't like for people to have a feeling that slaves are no more than dogs," said Squire Dowd, who wore a full-length suit. John Barker, in a vest and hat, was boastful that his family was from Madagascar. And Esther King Casey, hiding a little briar pipe she liked to smoke, recalled stories—nearly lost—that her grandmother told of the long, torturous crossing of the Atlantic.

"Who I is, how old I is, and where I is born, I don't know," said William Hamilton, who was abandoned as a child in the Deep South. Martin Jackson explained that few slaves bore a last name until the end of the war.

For most, slavery left lasting scars.

Jackson recalled exactly where his mother died.

"I can take you to the spot in the river today where she was drowned," he said. "She drowned herself. I never knew the reason behind it, but it was said she started to lose her mind and preferred death to that."

Betty Simmons remembered the day she was put on a boat in Memphis, Tennessee, and sent down the river to Mississippi and Louisiana. She knew that she had lost her family—"my people"—and would never see them again.

She never did.

And so many recalled blood.

"The blood would fly 'fore they was through with you," said Martin Ruffin, describing life at the hands of overseers. William Moore spoke of seeing blood "red up the ground." And Ben Horry talked about his mother—"my own Mama!"— lashed by a black overseer in a barn till her blood flowed.

"Blood! Christ! Yes, man. Listen to me. Lemme tell you what I see wid my eye now," said Horry.

He was made to stand and watch his mother being beaten.

"My own Daddy dere couldn't move," he said.

Years later, blood was still on the floor of the barn where his mother was beaten.

Blood. A river of blood.

THE SLAVE NARRATIVE COLLECTION compiled by the Works Progress Administration in the 1930s is the most significant effort to document slavery in the United States. Slave narratives—written accounts retelling the experience of the formerly enslaved—date back before the Revolutionary War. One of the first, *A Narrative of the Most Remarkable Particulars in the Life of James Albert Ukawsaw Gronniosaw*, tells the story of a 20-year-old African sold into slavery and shipped overseas. Like most narratives that came later, this was an eye-opening account that examined what was called the "peculiar institution."

"It is a generally received opinion, in England, that the natives of Africa go entirely unclothed," Gronniosaw wrote, "but this supposition is very unjust; they have a kind of dress so as to appear decent, though it is very slight and thin."

The book, published in the early 1770s, was a literary success and an international bestseller.

Dozens of slave narratives were written during the 1800s, published as books or pamphlets, particularly during the decades leading up to the Civil War. Most were exposés of slave life, often produced by abolitionist societies. They were meant to spur Northerners to take action against slavery. Southerners labeled them propagandistic political fiction.

Nat Turner, who led dozens of blacks in a rebellion against Virginia plantation owners, ending in a rampage that killed more than fifty white men, women and children, composed *The Confessions of Nat Turner* in 1831 from his prison cell before he was tried and executed. Frederick Douglass, who taught himself how to read and write, produced the masterpiece *Narrative of the Life of Frederick Douglass, an American Slave* in 1845. Eight years later, Solomon Northup wrote *Twelve Years a Slave.* "This is no fiction, no exaggeration," he wrote. "If I have failed in anything, it has been in presenting to the reader too prominently the bright side of the picture." More than 150 years later, his narrative, popular in its day, was made into the motion picture *12 Years a Slave.*

The slave narratives continued after the Civil War. The conclusion of the war ended the political *raison d'être* of the slave narrative, but formerly enslaved men and women continued to produce biographies and autobiographies.

In the late 1920s, author and anthropologist Zora Neale Hurston interviewed Cujo Lewis, who claimed to be the last survivor of the last slave ship sent from West Africa to the United States. "I want to know who you are," Hurston told Lewis, "and how you came to be a slave; and to what part of Africa do you belong, and how you fared as a slave, and how you have managed as a free man." Hurston couldn't find a publisher willing to print the book in Lewis' dialect, so the book sat unpublished—until 2018, when it was released as *Barracoon: The Story of the Last "Black Cargo."*

A new type of slave narrative—an effort to collect short interviews of formerly enslaved men and women—was started in the late 1920s by two professors at historically black colleges. Historian John B. Cade and his students at Southern University in Baton Rouge, Louisiana, interviewed 82 former slaves in 1929. Cade revived the work in the mid-1930s at Prairie View State College in Texas, where he directed the interviews of four hundred former slaves. At about the same time, sociologist Charles S. Johnson and researcher Ophelia Settle Egypt at Fisk University in Nashville, Tennessee, tracked down and talked to one hundred ex-slaves.

These oral interviews were indispensable because few of the enslaved left behind a written record.

"These documents herein made available, reveal some of the personal experiences of the slaves in the declining days of the institution," wrote the Fisk researchers. "They tell what the slaves saw and remembered; how they, themselves, or others whom they knew lived through the drudgery of menial work and the fear of the impending precarious world; how the slaves met their basic needs of sex, hunger and rest, within the very narrow confines of the system."

Historian Lawrence D. Reddick, one of Charles Johnson's students, convinced the Franklin Roosevelt administration to expand the effort. He and twelve black college graduates received a grant to interview 250 ex-slaves. Reddick envisioned a larger undertaking in which all the formerly enslaved living

420044

2 1937

WILLIS WINN claims to be 116
years old. He was born in
Louisiana, a slave of Bob Winn,
who Willis says taught him from
his youth that his birthday was
March 10, 1822. When he was
freed Willis and his father moved
to Hope, Askansas, where they
lived sixteen years. Willis then
moved to Texarkana and from there
to Marshall, where he has lived
fourteen years. Willis lives
alone in a one-room log house in
the rear of the Howard Vestal
home on the Powder Mill Road, north
of Marshall, and is supported by
an $11.00 per month old age pension.

"The onliest statement I can make 'bout my age is my old master,
Bob Winn, allus told me if anyone ask me how old I is to say I's borned
on March the tenth, in 1822. I's knowed my birthday since I's a shirt-
tail boy, but can't figure in my head.

"My pappy was Daniel Winn and he come from Alabama, and I 'member
him allus sayin' he'd like to go back there and get some chestnuts. Mammy
was named Patsy and they was nine of us chillen. The five boys was me
and Willie and Hosea and two Georges, and the gals was Car'lina and Dora
and Anna and Ada, and all us lived to be growed and have chillen.

"Massa Bob's house faced the quarters where he could hear us
holler when he blowed the big horn for us to git up. All the houses was
made of logs and we slept on shuck and grass mattresses what was allus full
of chinches. I still sleep on a grass mattress, 'cause I can't rest on
cotton and feather beds.

FIRST PAGE OF WILLIS WINN'S ORIGINAL TYPEWRITTEN INTERVIEW.

in the South would be interviewed. But the work was plagued by administrative and editorial problems. The larger project never took off.

Reddick's idea was revived in 1936 by the Federal Writers' Project, a branch of the Works Progress Administration. The WPA was a government agency set up to provide work to the one-quarter of Americans who were unemployed during the Great Depression. More than 8 million men and women were hired by the WPA to build roads, bridges, dams and parks—and to paint, sculpt and write. "Hell," said relief administrator Harry L. Hopkins, "artists have got to eat just like other people."

The WPA's Federal Writers' Project hired more than 6,500 unemployed writers, historians and teachers to gather the nation's history. They produced 48 books called *The American Guide* series for each state, as well as dozens of books and pamphlets on cities and regions. They also interviewed 10,000 ordinary Americans.

Federal Writers' Project managers were described as "romantic nationalists" because they were interested in the words and thoughts of almost everyone— from store clerks to prostitutes to meat packers. Everybody had something to say. The work of the government writers was a celebration of diversity and democracy.

In the course of gathering these life histories, WPA writers in Florida, Georgia, South Carolina and Virginia sought out and interviewed former slaves. In 1937, a few of these conversations were sent to the main Washington, D.C., office, where they caught the attention of John A. Lomax, who was in charge of gathering folklore (or word-of-mouth histories), and Sterling A. Brown, national editor of Negro affairs.

Lomax was a white anthropologist from Texas who called himself a ballad hunter. Starting in 1933, he worked for the Library of Congress hauling a bulky recorder with aluminum discs through the South to record old Negro melodies and the songs of rural whites. Four years later, he took charge of the Slave Narrative Collection.

The federal government's decision to embark on such a project was a crucial cultural moment for the United States. By seeking out elderly African Americans and recording their words, the government was declaring that the slave experience was fundamental to the history of America. The federal government's resolve to record these slave stories conferred a stronger sense of citizenship upon those who were interviewed. They were recognized.

Until that time, the history of slavery was primarily told by white historians—people like Georgia-born and -bred Ulrich Bonnell Phillips, whose monumental but one-sided 1918 book *American Negro Slavery* was based on the diaries and records of plantation owners. Phillips wrote about "generous masters" and slaves who were well-fed, well-clothed and carefully cared for in sickness. He wrote that work was fair and punishment was seldom cruel. He argued that slavery civilized and Christianized African Americans. His book fostered the plantation myth.

Phillips died two years before the start of the Slave Narrative Collection. He and most other historians of the age dismissed oral history, especially from the formerly enslaved, as unsubstantiated and inaccurate. Phillips called the memories of former slaves "unsafe."

But since then, historians have grown to value these memories.

The Federal Writers' Project interviews exploded the plantation myth. Who knew better how it felt to be a slave than slaves themselves?

As much as Lomax valued voice recordings, he realized from the start that these interviews must be carried out in the field with pen and paper. In April 1937, he sent instructions on how best to document the words of the formerly enslaved.

"The details of the interview should be reported as accurately as possible in the language of the original statements," Lomax recommended. "The writer should try to capture exactly what was said in the dialect of the subject," he wrote. "It should be remembered that the Federal Writers' Project is not interested in taking sides on any question. The worker should not censor any material collected, regardless of its nature."

Lomax sent a questionnaire to the writers that he recommended they use. It included twenty elementary questions: birth dates and locations, the names of parents, the type of work, the amount of food and clothing received, religion, reading, social life, sickness, freedom, marriage and life during and after the Civil War. The questionnaire was to be used as a guide.

Lomax never came up with an overall plan or scientific methodology for locating and interviewing former slaves. One former slave often directed writers to others. Because so many ex-slaves were interviewed, the narratives boast a remarkable assortment of stories about life on huge plantations and on tiny farms, about work in fields and in homes. Some appreciated their owners; some despised them. Some of the interviews were short—a couple of typewritten pages—and some rambled for dozens of pages. The interviewers found former slaves in 25 states and the District of Columbia.

But the Federal Writers' Project had a blind side. Whites dominated the agency. Only about one hundred of the five thousand writers and editors who worked at the project at any one time were black. Sterling A. Brown, one of the top editors, was a well-respected African American poet and scholar, but he had little influence beyond his editing of material that was directly linked to black Americans. And almost all of the interviews of the formerly enslaved outside of Florida, Georgia and Virginia were conducted by whites.

There is little doubt that the white writers carried bias and prejudice. They referred to their subjects as uncles and aunts, common nomenclature in the South in those days, and made detailed comments on the condition of their homes. W.F. Jordan wrote about Walter Calloway: "A glance at the interior of his cabin disclosed the fact that it was scrupulously neat and quite orderly in arrangement,

CHIMNEY OF ABANDONED
HOME, PUTNAM COUNTY,
GEORGIA, 1941.
IRVING RUSINOW PHOTO

AFRICAN AMERICAN CEMETERY NEAR PERSON COUNTY, NORTH CAROLINA, 1939. *DOROTHEA LANGE PHOTO*

a characteristic of a great many ex-slaves." Some writers mentioned how much they admired the docile aspects of their subjects. Wrote John Proctor Mills: "In Uncle Daniel Taylor we find the unusual, fast disappearing type of Negro ex-slave. (It makes the sentimental white man feel a deep sadness in the passing of these gentle old souls, whose lives have been well spent in serving to the best of their ability.)" And some interviewers made a point to note the racial features of their subjects. "Ben has straight hair, a Roman nose, and his speech is like that of the early white settler," wrote Florence Angermiller of Ben Kinchlow.

The few black writers usually quoted their subjects in standard English. White writers preferred to transcribe directly the "Negro dialect" that they heard. These interviewers were not trained linguists or ethnographers. John Mills was a songwriter; Gertha Couric ran a tearoom; and Mabel Farrior was a teacher, stenographer and bookkeeper. Some of the writers seemed to capture the language accurately; some, not so well. As one can see from the accompanying glossary, the phonetic spellings that were used were inconsistent.

What is important is that the thousands of interviews took place and that the elderly former slaves could remember details from their past lives so vividly and speak so eloquently.

The project to interview former slaves ended about 1938, when the Federal Writers' Project was reorganized and put back into the control of states. Benjamin A. Botkin, who took over for John Lomax as the project's folklore editor in 1938, was assigned to see that the 10,000 typewritten pages were organized and not forgotten. "History from the bottom up," he called them. "The best of the slave narratives also belongs to literature," Botkin wrote. He spent the next five years organizing them in the Reading Room at the Library of Congress—where they sat for decades.

THEN CAME HISTORIAN GEORGE P. RAWICK, who spent ten years copying the 10,000 pages at the Library of Congress to make them more accessible in his nineteen-volume set, *The American Slave: A Composite Autobiography.*

"I wanted to publish as much material by those who had been slaves as could be found in order to bury the nonsensical, elitist, and racist notion that there was no way of locating Afro-American slaves' accounts of their own experience," he wrote. The narratives gave a "full, rounded, and dynamic picture of the lives of slaves."

Each entry was important to Rawick, so he copied everything just as it was left. "I have also retained all the editorial marks, often, these marks reveal the differences among the interviewers, in terms of style and bias," he wrote. "In addition, I have retained the attempts at rending regional black speech dialects; no matter how inept these attempts may have been, they are evidence of a matter of considerable importance: the development of American speech."

When the volumes were released in 1972, Rawick thought his work was done. He had transcribed every page at the Library of Congress for his set of books, which were sent to hundreds of libraries across the United States, and had written a volume about what he had learned about slavery.

The following year, he was invited to speak at Tougaloo College in Jackson, Mississippi. His talk was well received, but afterward two colleagues suggested to Rawick that they all visit the nearby Mississippi Department of Archives and History to wade through WPA records. There they found thousands of pages of slave narratives that were never sent to Washington. That opened the floodgates. They found hundreds of new interviews, as well as extended versions of known interviews in the archives of 21 other states and the District of Columbia. By the time he was finished, Rawick published an additional 22 volumes of material (41 in total), which includes interviews of more than 3,500 formerly enslaved men and women.

In 2001, the Library of Congress posted the original 2,300 narratives online.

FELIX HAYWOOD WAS GROWING TIRED at the end of his interview when Felix Nixon, a writer who shared Haywood's first name, asked to snap his portrait. "At a request, he instantly got up and tapped his way out into the scorching sunshine to have his photograph taken," Nixon wrote. Sarah Colquitt told her interviewer, "I'd be proud to have my picture took."

Anne Maddox had to be wheeled out onto her front porch. Hagar Lewis crossed her arms. Bert Strong squinted into the sun. Squire Dowd, a former minister, posed with a Bible. Charles H. Anderson, a former soldier, sat with his Grand Army of the Republic service medals.

Bill Homer held still in front of the Fort Worth Courthouse and Ben Kinchlow positioned himself reaching toward leaves of corn on his Uvalde, Texas, property. Richard Toler stood ramrod straight on a cobblestone street in Cincinnati, and Orelia Alexie Franks stared out from among the billowing sheets on her laundry line in Beaumont, Texas.

Several men—Monroe Brackins, John W. Fields, Stepney Underwood and others—insisted on wearing a suit or part of a suit. Some women—Leithean Spinks, Martha Spence Bunton—chose to keep on their aprons.

About three hundred formerly enslaved men and women who were interviewed for the Federal Writers' Project were also photographed. It's not clear who or what was behind the photography, but the simple snapshot style is closely linked to the photo work of John Lomax and collaborator Ruby Pickens Tartt, an Alabama folklorist. The photos taken by the writers seemed to be almost an afterthought at the end of the interviews.

For some reason, the hundreds of photos taken for the Slave Narrative Collection had been largely overlooked. The negatives are missing and the slight impressions made by paperclips that attached the small prints to the typewritten interviews indicate that the photos were not particularly valued. The historian George Rawick, who faithfully sought out each draft of every interview, never bothered to reproduce any photographs.

The Library of Congress website includes most of the photographs taken for the Federal Writers' Project. The writers used inexpensive cameras, with limited focus and exposure control. They usually took only one photo of each subject. The pictures that were made were on standard stock paper. They were probably printed at drug stores.

These pictures—often grainy, frequently overexposed and frustratingly out of focus—are exceptionally straightforward. In most cases, the photographers stood with the sun at their back aiming directly toward their subject.

The subjects appeared to know how important these pictures were. They presented themselves with dignity and an awareness of who they were. They are sober and restrained and proud. Their portraits are explicit, authentic images that help reveal the toll of slavery.

The men and women in these photographs were not acquainted, but they share an essential bond: through their words and images they bear witness to this dark place in American history.

Editors' Note:

Excerpts used in this book are from Federal Writers' Project interviews with formerly enslaved men and women that were conducted during the late 1930s, more than seventy years after the Civil War. The people interviewed were in their seventies, eighties and nineties. A few thought they were more than a century old.

Their words come from two sources: the formal Slave Narrative Collection at the Library of Congress and from earlier drafts that were found during the 1970s in various state archives. Employees in individual state Federal Writers' Project offices were apparently directed to keep all drafts and send only the final version of each interview to Washington, D.C. These drafts are often longer and more detailed than the final narratives. Thousands of drafts were found by a team of historians and are part of the invaluable 22 volumes known as the supplement series of *The American Slave: A Composite Autobiography.*

Biographical information about those interviewed was also taken from the Slave Narrative Collection and the drafts. Additional biographical details were gathered from census records, marriage licenses, death records and contemporary newspaper accounts that were found online.

We wanted to be as faithful as possible to the original material—the Slave Narrative Collection and the drafts. The interviews have been excerpted, but we have used the exact transcriptions of the original interviews—only occasionally changing punctuation and paragraph order. The glossary on page 236 will help readers better understand the excerpts. We have used the word "nigger" because it was used by the former slaves themselves and was taken directly from the original source material. We understand the word can be shocking and offensive to read, but we felt it necessary to present the dialogue as transcribed.

Language matters. We never called an individual a "slave" because that designation does not describe their personhood. We always wrote they were "born into slavery" or "enslaved." We occasionally used the word "slave" when discussing enslaved people in general. We called plantation owners "slaveholders" rather than "slave owners."

The portrait photographs were taken by the interviewers from the Federal Writers' Project. The photos are in the possession of the Library of Congress. Credits for most of the pictures can be found on page 237. Professional government photographers who documented the South in the 1930s and 1940s took the pictures that start and end the book to set the scene. They worked for the Historic American Building Survey, Bureau of Agricultural Economics and Farm Security Administration. Their work can be found in the Library of Congress and the National Archives.

PART I

SLAVERY AND IDENTITY

INTERIOR OF OLD SLAVE QUARTERS NEAR
CARUTHERSVILLE, MISSOURI, 1936.
RUSSELL LEE PHOTO

'How could I forgit'

Do I 'member slavery days? Yes, suh! How could I forgit dem?

PENNY THOMPSON was one of nearly 4 million enslaved African Americans when she was born about 1852 on a plantation owned by Calvin Ingram in Coosa County, Alabama. The first captives from Africa arrived at Jamestown, Virginia, four centuries ago—in 1619. After the Civil War, she moved to Tyler, Texas, and married Ike Thompson. She was living in Fort Worth, Texas, when interviewed by the Federal Writers' Project in 1937.

I was born at Charleston, South Carolina, and at the age of two and a half years we landed at Luverne, Alabama, where with my mother I was sold for $400.

DANIEL TAYLOR was born into slavery about 1851. He and 1 million other enslaved people were forced to move from America's coastal states by slaveholders who relocated to larger, more fertile property in what would become known as the cotton kingdom. At the start of the Civil War, some of the plantation owners moved to stay ahead of advancing U.S. Army troops. After the war, Taylor worked as a janitor for the Montgomery City Schools in Alabama. He once pulled a teacher to safety during a school fire. That made him a hero.

Way back yonder my name was Mary Anne Burleson. I was bawn in Louisiana, but I don' know jes' where. I'se anywhere f'om 97 to 102 years old.

MARY ANNE BURLESON PATTERSON was born into slavery about 1840. She and her mother were forcibly moved to Texas, where they were sold to Aaron Burleson, of Rogers Hill near Austin. The names of enslaved people were not recorded in the nation's census until 1870, so information that predates the Civil War is scant. After the war, she married Alex Patterson. They farmed and raised fifteen children.

In de year of 1860, Missy Mary gits married to Bill Johnson and at dat weddin' Massa Homer gives me and 49 other niggers to her for de weddin' present. Massa Johnson's father gives him 50 niggers, too.

Dey has a gran' weddin'.

BILL HOMER was born into slavery in 1850 on a plantation owned by Jack Homer in Shreveport, Louisiana, and was forcibly moved to Caldwell, Texas. Enslaved people like Homer were treated as property. They and their children were owned for life unless they escaped, were sold or set free. Most were sold at least once. After the war, Homer married Mary Robinson, raised fourteen children and worked as a rancher and farmer until 1935. He was interviewed in Fort Worth.

In those days, there were men who made a business of buying up Negroes at auction sales and shipping them down to New Orleans to be sold to owners of cotton and sugar cane plantations. Just as men today buy and ship cattle.

These men were called nigger traders, and they would ship whole boatloads at a time, buying them up, two or three here, two or three there, and holding them in a jail until they had a boatload.

This practice gave rise to the expression "sold down the river."

MARY CRANE, daughter of Violet Copher, was born into slavery in 1855 on a farm owned by Wattie Williams in Larue County, Kentucky. Her father joined the U.S. Army after the ban against African Americans was lifted. More than 200,000 African Americans served in the U.S. Army and Navy during the Civil War. She married and raised four children. She was living in Mitchell, Indiana, when interviewed.

I've saw lots of slaves bid off like stock and babies sold from their mammy's breast. Some brung 'bout $1,500 owing to how strong they is.

Spec'lators used to ride all over the country near our place and buy up niggers. And I've saw as many as fifty in a gang, like convicts.

REEVES TUCKER, son of Winnie and Armistead Tucker, was born into slavery about 1839 on a plantation owned by George Washington Tucker Sr. in Bibb County, Alabama. At age six, Reeves was forcibly moved to Gilmer, Texas, following the death of his slaveholder. He married Mary Tanglin and raised eight children. They farmed most of their life near Marshall, Texas. He died in 1938.

You see, dere was traders dat traveled from place to place dem days and dey takes sometimes as much as 100 niggers for to trade. Dere was sheds outside of town, whar dey keeps de niggers when dey comes to town.

At de auction I'se seen dem sell a family. Maybe one man buy de mammy, anudder buy de pappy and anudder buy all de chillens or maybe jus' one, like dat.

I'se see dem cry like dey at de funeral when dey am parted. Dey has to drag 'em away.

JAMES BROWN, son of John Brown, was born into slavery in 1853 on a farm owned by George Burney in Bell County, Texas. James and his mother were sold to John Blair, a farmer in nearby Waco. Following the war, he worked as a coachman, a farmer and in a lumberyard. He lost his sight in the 1920s and had no living relatives. He lived in a small house in Fort Worth.

We sees others sol' on the auction block. They're put in stalls like pens for cattle and there's a curtain, sometimes just a sheet in front of them so the bidders can't see the stock too soon. The overseer's standin' just outside with a big black snake whip and a pepper box pistol in his hand.

Then they pulls the curtain up and the bidders crowds 'round. The overseer tells the age of the slaves and what they can do. One bidder takes a pair of white gloves they have and rubs his fingers over a man's teeth, and he says, "You say this buck's 20 years old, but there's cups worn to his teeth. He's 40 years if he's a day."

So they knock that buck down for $1,000, 'cause they calls the men "bucks" and the women "wenches." Then the overseer makes 'em walk across the platform. He makes 'em hop; he makes 'em trot; he makes 'em jump.

JAMES MARTIN, son of Lizzie and Preston Martin, was born into slavery about 1847 in Alexandria, Virginia. Preston Martin was freed at the age of sixteen and spent $1,200 to purchase Lizzie's freedom so they could marry. Their teenage son James was impressed into the Confederate Army and later served in the U.S. Army fighting Native Americans in the Guadalupe Mountains in western Texas. After his discharge, he worked for the railroads and drove cattle near San Antonio. He died in 1946.

I seed chillun too lil' to walk from dey mammies sol' right off de block in Woodville. Dey was sol' jus' like calfs.

JOSIE BROWN, daughter of Keyia and Reuben Heard, was born into slavery about 1859 on a plantation owned by George Heard in Victoria, Texas. Her mother was a Choctaw Indian who was kidnapped and sold into slavery. Hundreds of thousands of American Indians were enslaved by Europeans starting in the Colonial Period—and Indians later enslaved blacks. Brown married twice and raised ten children. She also cared for six or seven orphans. She lived in Woodville, Texas, and died in 1949.

Dey have the big warehouse in places like Memphis, and take the nigger the day befo' the sale and give him plenty to eat to make him look in good humor. They chain him up the night befo' the sale, and iffen he am the fightin' nigger, they handcuffs him.

The auctioneer say, "Dis nigger am eighteen year old, sound as the dollar, can pick 300 pounds of cotton a day, good disposition, easy to manage, come up 'xamine him."

They strips him to the waist and everybody look him over and the good ones brung $1,500 sometimes.

JOSH MILES was born into slavery about 1859 on a plantation owned by the Miles family in Richmond, Virginia. In 1862, the slaveholders moved their plantation to Franklin, Texas. After the Civil War, Josh Miles helped build the railroad line for the International & Great Northern from Houston to Waco. Laid off because of old age, he lived in Mart, Texas.

I stays with Miss Olivia till '63 when Mr. Will set us all free. I was 'bout seventeen year old then or more. I say I goin' find my mamma [who was sold and sent to Texas].

Mr. Will fixes me up two papers, one 'bout a yard long and the other some smaller, but both has big, gold seals what he says is the seal of the State of Missouri.

He gives me money and buys my fare ticket to Texas, and tells me they is still slave times down here and to put the papers in my bosom, but to do whatever the white folks tells me, even if they wants to sell me. But he say, "'Fore you gets off the block, jes' pull out the papers, but jes' hold 'em up to let folks see, and don't let 'em out of your hands. And when they sees them they has to let you alone."

A man asks me where I goin' and says to come 'long, and he takes me to a Mr. Charley Crosby. They takes me to the block what they sells slaves on. I gets right up like they tells me, 'cause I 'lects what Mr. Will done told me to do. And they starts biddin' on me. And when they cried off and this Mr. Crosby comes up to get me, I jes' pulled out my papers and helt 'em up high. And when he sees 'em, he say, "Let me see them." But I says, "You jes' look at it up here."

And he squints up and say, "This gal am free and has papers."

MARY ARMSTRONG, daughter of Siby and Sam Adams, was born into slavery about 1846 on a farm owned by Polly and William Cleveland near St. Louis, Missouri. Armstrong was presented as a gift to the Clevelands' daughter, Olivia, and her husband, Will Adams, who set her free in 1863. Thousands of African Americans roamed the South at the end of the war searching for their families that had been split apart. All free blacks—in the North and the South—were required by law to carry detailed freedom papers to prove their status. Armstrong found her mother near Wharton, Texas, after the war. She married John Armstrong and lived in Houston.

You see there was slave traders in those days, jes' like you got horse and mule and auto traders now. They bought and sold slaves and hired them out. Yes'm, rented them out. "Allotted" means somethin' like hired out. But the slave never got no wages. That all went to the master. The man they was allotted to paid the master.

I never was sold. My mama was sold only once, but she was hired out many times. Yes'm when a slave was allotted, somebody made a down payment and gave a mortgage for the rest. A chattel mortgage.

Times don't change, just the merchandise.

SARAH FRANCES SHAW GRAVES, daughter of Virginia and Pratt Barber, was born into slavery in 1850 near Louisville, Kentucky. She and her mother were forcibly moved to Missouri to work for another slaveholder. Her father, never again seen by the family, was left behind in Kentucky. She married Joseph Hartzel Graves and raised one son. They bought 120 acres of farmland near Skidmore, Missouri, where she was interviewed. She died in 1942.

Marster William raises de corn and rice and wheat and barley and vegetables and honey and lots of cotton. Dey works animals, de mules and de oxen, but I seed de niggers hitched to de plow sometimes.

De small chillens is kep' dere and de marster sho' am 'ticular 'bout dem. Lots of times he look dem over and say, "Dat one be worth a t'ousand dollars," or "Dat one be a whopper." You see, 'twas jus' like raisin' young mules.

On that plantation, dere am no weddin' 'lowed for to git married. They jus' gits married, but some not 'lowed to git married 'cause the master anxious to raise good, big niggers, the kind what am able to do lots of work and sell for a heap of money. Him have 'bout ten wenches. Him not 'low to git married. . . . That nigger do no work but watch them womens and he am the husban' for them all.

De Master sho' was a-raisin' some fine niggers that way.

WILLIE WILLIAMS was born into slavery about 1860 on a plantation owned by William Maddox near Sparta, Louisiana. Maddox sold his plantation in 1868 and moved with Williams to Fort Worth, Texas. Williams worked at the Maddox Milk and Ice Company for decades. It's unclear whether he ever married. Enslaved men and women were not allowed to be legally married, although unofficial wedding ceremonies—sometimes culminated by "jumping the broom"—were often encouraged by slaveholders.

After [our] weddin', we went down to de cabin. . . . But Exter couldn' stay no longer den dat night kaze he belonged to Marse Snipes Durham an' he had to back home. He lef' de nex' day for his plantation, but he come back every Saturday night an' stay 'twell Sunday night.

I was glad when de war stopped kaze den me an' Exter could be together all de time 'stead of Saturday an' Sunday.

We had eleven chillun. Nine was bawn befo' surrender and two after we was set free. So I had two chillun that wuzn' bawn in bondage. I was worth a heap to Marse George kaze I had so manny chillun.

The more chillun a slave had the more they was worth.

TEMPIE HERNDON DURHAM was born into slavery about 1834 on a plantation owned by Betsy and George Herndon in Chatham County, North Carolina. On average, enslaved mothers gave birth to between nine and ten children. Tempie informally married Exter Durham, who lived on a neighboring plantation. After the war, they rented and purchased a farm. She lived in Durham, North Carolina, and died in 1938.

My pappy have twelve children by my mammy and twelve by anudder nigger name Mary. You keep the count.

Then dere am Liza, him have ten by her. And dere am Mandy, him have eight by her. And dere am Betty, him have six by her. Now, let me 'lect some more. I can't bring the names to mind, but dere am two or three other what have jus' one or two children by my pappy. That am right. Close to fifty children, 'cause my mammy done told me. It's disaway: my pappy am the breedin' nigger.

You sees, when I meets a nigger on that plantation, I's most sho' it am a brudder or sister, so I don't try keep track of 'em.

LEWIS JONES was born into slavery in 1851 on a plantation owned by Fred Tate in Fayette County, Texas. After the war, he took his father's name and worked at a cotton gin factory in nearby La Grange. He moved to Fort Worth to work for Armour & Company, married Jane Owen and raised three children.

Negro women having children by the masters was common. My relatives on my mother's side, who were Kellys, are mixed blooded. They are partly white. We, the darkies, and many of the whites hate that a situation like this exists.

SQUIRE DOWD, son of Jennie Dowd and Elias Kennedy, was born into slavery in 1855 on a plantation owned by Ann Marie and Willis Dickerson Dowd near Carthage, North Carolina. Squire Dowd's observation was accurate: more than one in three African American men descend from a white male ancestor—who most likely fathered their children through forced sex during slave days. After the war, Dowd was ordained a Christian minister and moved to nearby Raleigh. He married Anna Matthews and raised one daughter. He died in 1945.

When I was six years old, all of us children were taken from my parents because my master died and his estate had to be settled. We slaves were divided by this method.

Three disinterested persons were chosen to come to the plantation, and together they wrote the names of the different heirs on a few slips of paper. These slips were put in a hat and passed among us slaves. Each one took a slip, and the name on the slip was the new owner. I happened to draw the name of a relative of my master, who was a widow.

I can't describe the heartbreak and horror of that separation. I was only six years old and it was the last time I ever saw my mother for longer than one night.

JOHN M. FIELDS, listed as John W. Fields in the government's Slave Narratives, was the son of Sarah McFarland and Obediah Fields. He was born into slavery about 1848 in Owensboro, Kentucky. He escaped in 1864 and attempted to join the Union Army but was refused because of his age. Fields moved to Lafayette, Indiana, and worked as a laborer and household servant. He married Elizabeth and raised four children. He died in 1953.

PART II

DAY TO DAY

OLD PLANTATION HOUSE,
PUTNAM COUNTY, GEORGIA, 1941.
IRVING RUSINOW PHOTO

'It was hell'

If you's wants to know 'bout slavery time, it was hell.

CARTER J. JOHNSON, listed as Carter J. Jackson, was the son of Charlotte and Charles Johnson. He was born into slavery about 1853 on a plantation owned by Parson George Rogers in Montgomery, Alabama. Carter Johnson served as a personal assistant to Rogers' son in the Confederate Army until the son was killed in the 1862 Battle of Shiloh in Tennessee. Young Carter was returned to the Rogers plantation and was forcibly moved with forty other enslaved people to Texas. After the war, he married Sallie Gray and raised seven children. He helped build a thirty-mile railroad line from Longview to Big Sandy, Texas. He was interviewed in Tatum, Texas, and died in 1940.

Lots of old slaves closes the door before they tell the truth about their days of slavery. When the door is open, they tell how kind their masters was and how rosy it all was. You can't blame them for this because they had plenty of early discipline, making them cautious about saying anything uncomplimentary about their masters.

I, myself, was in a little different position than most slaves and, as a consequence, have no grudges or resentment. However, I can tell you the life of the average slave was not rosy. They were dealt out plenty of cruel suffering.

Even with my good treatment, I spent most of my time planning and thinking of running away. I could have done it easy, but my old father used to say, "No use running from bad to worse, hunting better."

MARTIN JACKSON was born into slavery about 1847 on a plantation owned by Alvy Fitzpatrick in Victoria County, Texas. Jackson served in the Civil War and World War I as a medic and cook. After the war, he married Sarah Flint and raised fifteen children. He lost his sight in the 1920s while living in San Antonio. His 1940 obituary noted that Jackson was "one of the section's best cowboys."

Massa Thompson had a awful big plantation and more'n 300 cullud folks and three rows of cabins 'bout two blocks long, and 'bout one family to a cabin. No floors in dem cabins. You stands on dirt and de furniture am something you knows ain't there. Why man, there am jus' benches to sit on and a homemake table and bunks.

De bell am rung when meal time comes and all de slaves lines up with their pans and cups and passes de service table. And de food am put on dere pans and milk in de cup. Dat de one time massa could allus 'pend on de niggers. When de bell say, "Come and git it," all us am there. Us takes de food to de cabins and eats it.

Us have plenty hawg meat and veg'tables and butter and 'lasses and honey. De food ain't short no time 'round massa 'cause he say niggers works better when dey feeds good.

LEITHEAN SPINKS was born into slavery in 1855 on a plantation owned by Fay Thompson in Rankin County, Mississippi. Her memories were accurate: some enslaved people were fed well; some nearly starved because food was rationed. Spinks was forcibly moved as a child to East Feliciana Parish, Louisiana. She married twice and raised eight children. She lived with her daughter in Fort Worth.

Ah never had no good times till ah was free.

Ah nevah went to school. Learned to read and write mah name
after ah was free in night school. But they nevah allowed us
to have a book in ouah hand and we couldn't have no money,
neither. If we had money, we had to tu'n it ovah to ouah ownah.
Chu'ch was not allowed in ouah pa't, neithah.

We was nevah allowed no pa'ties, and when they had goin' ons
at the big house, we had to clear out. Ah had to wo'k hard all the
time every day in the week.

We had very bad eatin'. Bread, meat, water. And they fed it to us in
a trough, jes' like the hogs. . . . And the flo' in ouah cabin was dirt,
and at night we'd jes' take a blanket and lay down on the flo'. The
dog was supe'ior to us; they would take him in the house.

RICHARD TOLER, son of Lucy and George Washington Toler, was born into slavery about 1837 on
a plantation owned by Henry Toler near Lynchburg, Virginia. Richard Toler moved to Cincinnati,
Ohio, after the war and worked as a blacksmith, stonemason and carpenter. He married three
times and raised six children.

When I was a boy, I wo'e what was called shirt-tail. It was a long, loose shirt with no pants. I did not wear pants until I was about ten or twelve.

BEN KINCHLOW, son of Lizaer Moore and Lad Kinchlow, was born into slavery in 1846 on a plantation owned by Sandy Moore in Wharton County, Texas. Enslaved fieldworkers like Kinchlow were allotted simple, drab work clothes made up of inexpensive linens. Kinchlow, his mother and brother were set free when he was a child. After the war, he worked as a ranch hand, married Elisa Dawson and raised six children in a small house in Uvalde, Texas. He died in 1942.

Befo' I's a sizeable child, mammy took sick with diphtheria and died, and pappy had to be mammy and pappy to us. Pappy was a big-bodied man and on Sunday mornin' he'd git out of bed and make a big fire and say, "Jiminy cripes! You chillen stay in you beds and I'll make de biscuits." He would, too.

Dey sho' was big biscuits, but dey was good. We never did git no butter, though.

MARTHA SPENCE BUNTON was born into slavery on New Year's Day of 1856 on a plantation owned by John Bell in Murfreesboro, Tennessee. She, her mother and four sisters were sold to Joseph Spence, who forcibly moved the family to Montopolis, Texas, now part of Austin. The new holder purchased Martha's father, who was owned by another slaveholder in Tennessee. After the war, Martha Spence married Andy Bunton, a farmer, and raised nine children. She was living with her sister in 1937 on a twelve-acre farm east of Austin.

Some pore niggers were half starved.

They belonged to other people. Missus Mary would call them in to feed 'em, see them outside the fence pickin' up scraps. They'd call out at night, "Marse John, Marse John." They's afraid to come in daytime. Marse John'd say, "What's the matter now?" They'd say, "I'se hongry." He'd say, "Come in and git it." He'd cure lots of meat, for we'd hear them hollerin' at night when they'd beat the pore niggers for beggin' or stealin', or some crime.

Some whites had a dark hole in the ground. A "dungeon" they called it, to put their slaves in. They'd carry them bread and water once a day. I'se afraid of the hole. They'd tell me the devil was in that hole.

HAGAR LEWIS, the youngest of Lize McFarland's sixteen children, was born into slavery in 1855 on the Martin plantation near Tyler, Texas. Her father was enslaved on a nearby farm. She was delivered along with her mother and siblings as a wedding gift to Mary Martin and John McFarland. After the war, she married A. Lewis and moved to San Antonio. Her husband died young; she raised two sons. One, an electrical engineer, supported her in El Paso.

Our houses was lak horse stables, made of logs wid mud an' sticks dobbed in de cracks. Dey had no floors. Dere warn't no furniture 'cept a box fer de dresser wid a piece of looking glass to look in. Us had to sleep on shuck mattresses an' us cooked on big fireplaces wid long hooks out over de fire to hang pots on to bile.

Bout four o'clock in de evenin' all de little niggers was called up in de big yard where de cook had put milk in a long wooden trough an' crumbled ash cake in it. Us had potlicker in de trough, too. Us et de bread an' milk wid shells an' would use our hands—but it was good.

ANNE MADDOX, daughter of Rhody and Charlie Heath, was born into slavery before the war on a plantation owned by John Umford in Virginia. She was sold to Bill Maddox of Alabama. She married Doc Maddox and raised five children. She was living with her youngest child in a small cabin in Opelika, Alabama, in 1937 and died that year.

The slaves what worked in the fields was woke up 'fore light with a horn and worked till dark. And then there was the stock to tend to and cloth to weave. The overseer come 'round at nine o'clock to see if all is in the bed, and then go back to his own house. When us knowed he's sound asleep, we'd slip out and run 'round sometimes. They locked the young men up in a house at night and on Sunday to keep 'em from runnin' 'round.

We slips off and have prayer but daren't 'low the white folks know it. And sometime we hums 'ligious songs low like when we's workin'. It was our way of prayin' to be free, but the white folks didn't know it.

MILLIE ANN SMITH was born into slavery in 1850 on a plantation owned by George Washington Trammell in Rusk County, Texas. Before her birth, Trammell bought her mother and three siblings from a Mississippi enslaver, leaving behind her father. He ran away, found his family in Texas and convinced Trammell to purchase him. Not all slaveholders prohibited religion as Trammell did. Some believed it offered hope and made for better workers. After the war, Millie Ann lived with her parents until she married Tom Smith. They raised five children.

Us pick 'bout 100 pound cotton in one basket. I didn't mind pickin' cotton, 'cause I never did have de backache. I pick two and three hunnert pounds a day, and one day I picked 400. Sometime de prize give by massa to de slave what pick de most. De prize am a big cake or some clothes.

MARY ANNE KINCHEON EDWARDS was born into slavery before the Civil War on a plantation owned by the Kincheon family in Baton Rouge, Louisiana. She was sold to Felix Vaughn, who forcibly moved her to Texas. More than half of all enslaved people in the South worked on cotton plantations, usually in large labor gangs organized and supervised by plantation owners or their white overseers. After the war, Mary Anne Kincheon married Osburn Edwards and raised five children. She lived in Austin.

I never seed ma and pa much 'cept on Sundays. Dey was allus workin' in de fields, an' I was out chasin' rabbits an' sech mos' of de time. At night, I jest et my cornpone an' drink my buttermilk an' fell on de bed asleep.

MAUGAN SHEPHERD, son of Betsy and Bunk Wiley, was born into slavery before 1857 on a plantation owned by Rich Wiley in Chestnut Hill, Alabama. Enslaved adults were expected to harvest between 150 and 200 pounds of cotton a day. They worked from early morning until well past dusk except on Sundays during much of the year. After freedom, Shepherd married a woman named Kitty. He was working as a yardman in 1937 in nearby Eufaula when he was interviewed.

I had two little mistises 'bout as old as me, and I played wid dem all de time and slep' on a pallet in dey room ev'y night. Dey slep' on de big bed.

LIZZIE HILL, born about 1843, was enslaved by Richard Dozier and his wife near Cuthbert, Georgia. Hill's recollection was not uncommon: enslaved boys and girls were allowed to play with the slaveholders' children. White boys and girls usually took the role of superiors. Hill worked in Eufaula, Alabama, as a laundress. She was living in the home of her niece in 1937.

Miss Lee have a china doll with a wreath of roses round it head. We takes turns playin' with it. I had a rag doll, and it jes' a bundle of rags with strings tied round it to give it a shape.

EMMA WATSON, daughter of Lucindy Lane, was born into slavery about 1852. A Mississippi plantation owner sold Lane to Carl Forrester in Ellis County, Texas, just before Emma's birth, leaving the girl's father behind. She married after the war, worked as a sharecropper, raised four children and was living with her daughter in 1937 in Dallas.

Our clothes were bad and beds were sorry. We went barefooted in a way. What I mean by that is that we had shoes part of the time. We got one pair o' shoes a year. When dey wored out, we went barefooted. Sometimes we tied them up with strings, and they were so ragged de tracks looked like bird tracks where we walked in the road. We were compelled to walk about at night to live. We were so hungry we were bound to steal or parish. This trait seems to be handed down from slavery days.

LOUISA ADAMS, daughter of Easter and Jacob Covington, was born into slavery about 1857 on a plantation owned by Emma and Tom Covington in Rockingham, North Carolina. She married James Adams after the war and raised one child. She was interviewed in North Carolina.

We has parties and sings:

> "Massa sleeps in de feather bed,
> Nigger sleeps on de floor;
> When we'uns gits to Heaven,
> Dey'll be no slaves no more."

MILLIE WILLIAMS, daughter of Martha Birdon and Milton Wade, was born in 1851 on a plantation owned by Joe Benford in Tennessee. She was sold as a baby along with her mother, but Millie was soon returned to Benford without her mother. He put her on the auction block at age seven and sold her to Bill Dunn, who forcibly moved her to Texas. He traded her for land. After the war, Williams moved to Dallas. She married twice and lived in Fort Worth.

PART III

TRAUMA THAT LASTS FOREVER

SLAVE QUARTERS AND WOODHOUSE,
CECIL COUNTY, MARYLAND, 1936.
E.H. PICKERING PHOTO

'Rules for the slaves'

They had rules for the slaves to be governed by and they were whipped when they disobeyed.

ALMONT M. MOORE, son of Anna and Jiles D. Moore, was born into slavery about 1846 on a plantation owned by Lucinda and W.R. Sherrad near Marshall, Texas. Moore's observation was factual: far more than half of the men and women interviewed for the Slave Narratives said they were whipped. After the war, he attended Bishop and Wiley colleges, two historically black colleges in Marshall, received a teacher's certificate and worked as an instructor and preacher. He married and raised six children. In 1937, he was living on a farm that was part of the former Sherrad plantation.

Whip the slaves? Oh, my God! Don't mention it; don't mention it! Lots of them in Old Dominion got beatings for punishment. They didn't have no jail for slaves, but the owners used a whip and lash on 'em.

CHARLES H. ANDERSON was born into slavery in 1845 in a home owned by J.L. Woodson in Richmond, Virginia, a state known as Old Dominion. Floggings such as those he witnessed were public displays, often administered after acts of resistance. The enslaved resisted: they slowed work, hid, feigned ignorance and confronted their slaveholders. After the Civil War, Anderson served as a construction manager for the Chesapeake and Ohio Railway. He married Helen Comer and raised two children. He was living with his stepdaughter in 1937 in Cincinnati.

Some white folks might want to put me back in slavery if I tells how we was used in slavery time, but you asks me for the truth.

The overseer was 'straddle his big horse at three o'clock in the mornin', roustin' the hands off to the field. He got them all lined up and then come back to the house for breakfas'.

The rows was a mile long, and no matter how much grass was in them, if you leaves one sprig on your row they beats you nearly to death. Lots of times they weighed cotton by candlelight. All the hands took dinner to the field in buckets, and the overseer give them fifteen minutes to git dinner. He'd start cuffin' some of them over the head when it was time to stop eatin' and go back to work. He'd go to the house and eat his dinner, and then he'd come back and look in all the buckets. And if a piece of anything that was there when he left was et, he'd say you was losin' time and had to be whipped.

He'd drive four stakes in the ground, and tie a nigger down and beat him till he's raw. Then he'd take a brick and grind it up in a powder and mix it with lard and put it all over him and roll him in a sheet. It'd be two days or more 'fore that nigger could work 'gain.

WES BRADY, son of Harriet Ellis and Peter Calloway, was born into slavery in 1849 on a plantation owned by John Jeems in Harrison County, Texas. After freedom, Brady and his mother farmed. He spent most of his life in East Texas, and was living with friends near Marshall in 1937.

There was plenty white folks dat was sho bad to de niggers, and specially dem overseers.

A nigger whut lived on the plantation jinin' ours shot and killed an overseer. Den he run 'way. He come to de river and seed a white man on udder side and say, "Come and git me." Well, when dey got him, dey found out whut he'd done and was gwine to burn him 'live.

Jedge Clements, the man dat keep law and order, say he wouldn't burn a dog 'live. So he lef'.

But dey sho burn dat nigger 'live for I seed him atter he was burned up.

MARTHA BRADLEY was born into slavery about 1837 on a plantation owned by a doctor named Lucas in Montgomery County, Alabama. Slaveholders, liked the one Bradley recounted, hired overseers to get the most work out of enslaved workers. No limits were placed on the kind of discipline they could employ. In 1937, a century after her birth, Bradley was living in Montgomery.

The first work I done in slavery was totin' water and dinner to the field hands in gourd buckets. We didn't have tin buckets then. The hands worked from sun to sun, and if the overseer seed 'em slackin' up he cussed 'em and sometimes whacked 'em with a bullwhip.

I seed 'em whipped till their shirt stuck to their back. I seed my mammy whipped for shoutin' at white folks meetin'. Old massa stripped her to the waist and whipped her with a bullwhip. Heaps of 'em was whipped jus' 'cause they could be whipped. Some owners half fed their hands and then whipped them for beggin' for grub.

SOL WALTON, whose mother was named Helen, was born into slavery in 1849 on a plantation owned by Mary and Sam Lampkin in Mobile, Alabama. After the war, Walton and his father sharecropped near Mooringsport, Louisiana. He moved to Marshall, Texas, to farm and worked for the Texas & Pacific Railway. He married Liza Montecue and raised eight children.

Massa John am de kind massa and don't have whuppin's. He tell de overseer, "If you can't make dem niggers work without de whup, den you not de man I wants."

Mos' de niggers 'have theyselves. And when dey don't, massa put dem in de li'l house what he call de jail with nothin' to eat till deys ready to do what he say.

PAULINE GRICE was born into slavery about 1856 on a plantation owned by John Blackshier near Atlanta, Georgia. Private jails or dungeons, like the one she recalled, were not uncommon on large plantations. After the Civil War, Pauline worked with her mother and her mother's new husband as sharecroppers. She married Robert Grice and raised two children on a Texas truck farm. She died in 1937, soon after her interview.

The Cavins allus thunk lots of their niggers, and Grandma Maria say, "Why shouldn't they—it was their money."

WILL ADAMS, son of Amelia and Freeman Cavin, was born into slavery in 1857 on a plantation owned by Dave Cavin in Harrison County, Texas. Adams spent twenty years working there after the Civil War. He left to farm and do odd jobs in Marshall. He and his wife raised ten children.

Honey, all the white folks wan't good to dere slaves. I's seen po' niggers 'mos' tore up by dogs and whupped 'tell they bled w'en they did'n' do lak the white folks say.

CHARITY ANDERSON was born into slavery about 1836 in Bell's Landing, Alabama. She was enslaved by Leslie Johnson, who ran a tavern for river steamer passengers. Married with children, Anderson did domestic work—washing, ironing and weaving—after the war. She lived in Toulminville, now a neighborhood of Mobile.

We is heared slaves on farms close by hollerin' when they git beat. Some the neighbors works they hands till ten at night, and weighed the last weighin' by candles. If the day's pickin' wasn't good 'nough, they beat them till it a pity.

BERT STRONG was born into slavery in 1864 on a plantation owned by Dave Cavin in Harrison County, Texas. He and his mother lived there for ten years after the war. Strong then farmed nearby, married a woman named Anna and raised two children. He lived near Marshall.

The niggers sung songs in the field when they was feeling good and wasn't scart of old massa. Sometime they'd slack up on that hoe and old massa holler, "I's watchin' yous." The hands say, "Yas, suh, us sees you, too." Then they brightened up on that hoe.

The overseer was named Charley, and there was one driver to see everyone done his task. If he didn't, they fixed him up. Them what fed the stock got up at three, and the overseer would tap a bell so many times to make 'em git up. The rest got up at four and worked till good dark. They'd give us a hundred lashes for not doing our task. The overseer put five men on you—one on each hand, one on each foot, and one to hold your head down to the ground. You couldn't do anything but wiggle. The blood would fly 'fore they was through with you.

MARTIN RUFFIN, son of Cynthia and Will Ruffin, was born into slavery about 1854 on a plantation owned by Josh Perry near Port Caddo, Texas. He stayed until 1876, when he and his parents moved to a farm. He relocated to Marshall, where he cooked in hotels and cafes. He married Lula Downs and raised five children.

We lives close to the meanest owner in the country. Our massa wouldn't keep no overseer, 'cause he say his niggers wasn't dogs. But dis other man, he keeps overseers to beat the niggers, and he has the big leather bullwhip with lead in the end—and he beats some slaves to death.

We heared them holler and holler till they couldn't holler no mo! Then they jes' sorta grunt every lick till they die. We finds big streams of blood where he has whooped them. And when it rained the whole top of the ground jes' looks like a river of blood dere.

Sometime he bury he niggers, and sometime the law come out and make him bury dem. He put them in chains and stockades and sometimes he would buck and gag dem.

De mamas what expectin' babies was whooped to make them work faster. And when babies was sick, they has to put them in the basket on top dere heads and take them to the cotton patch, and put them under the cotton stalks and try to 'tend to dem.

Lawd, Lawd, them was awful times.

LOU WILLIAMS was born into slavery about 1829 on a plantation owned by Abram and Kitty Williams in southern Maryland. From the age of five until the Civil War, she served as a nursemaid to the Williams' children. She then moved to Louisiana to work as a cook. She married and raised one child. When interviewed, she was living with a grandchild in San Angelo, Texas.

I heered my mammy say she knowed a slave woman what owned by Massa Rickets, and she workin' in the field, and she heavy with the chile what not born yet, and she has to set down in the row to rest.

She was havin' the misery and couldn't work good, and the boss man had a nigger dig a pit where her stomach fit in, and lay her down and tie her so she can't squirm 'round none, and flog her till she lose her mind.

Yes, suh, that the truf.

My mammy say she knowed that woman a long time after dat, and she never right in the head 'gain.

VAN MOORE, son of Mary and Tom Moore, was born into slavery about 1857 on a plantation owned by the Cunningham family near Lynchburg, Virginia. What he saw in the fields was not unique. On some plantations, women were removed from fieldwork early in their pregnancy. But on others, they were expected to work until a week before they were to give birth. Van Moore's parents were enslaved on nearby plantations in central Virginia. Their slaveholders, who were related, both moved their plantations to Texas when he was a baby. His family reunited after the war. Moore lived in Houston.

Miss Mary was good to us, but us had to work hard and late. I worked in the fields every day from 'fore daylight to almost plumb dark. I usta take my littlest baby wid me. I had two chilluns, and I'd tie hit up to a tree limb to keep off the ants and bugs whilst I hoed and worked the furrow.

SARA COLQUITT was born into slavery about 1837 on a plantation owned by Bill and Mary Slaughter in Richmond, Virginia. She was sold on the block for $1,000 at Hill, Alabama, to Sam Rainey. New mothers, like Colquitt, were expected to return to the field as soon as two or three weeks after childbirth. She married Prince Hodnett and raised two children. She was living with her daughter, Eli, in Opelika, Alabama, in 1937.

Yes, suh, they whupped pow'ful hard sometimes. My mammy gits whupped one time 'cause she come from the fiel' for to nuss her baby, and once for the cause she don' keep up her row in the fiel'.

One day, I remembers my brother January was cotched ober seein' a gal on the next plantation. He had a pass but the time on it done gib out.

Well suh, when the massa found out that he was a hour late, he got as mad as a hive of bees. So when brother January he come home, the massa took down his long mule skinner and tied him wid a rope to a pine tree. He strip' his shirt off and said, "Now, nigger, I'm goin' to teach you some sense."

Wid that he started layin' on the lashes. January was a big, fine lookin' nigger; the finest I ever seed. He was jus' four years older dan me. And when the massa begin a beatin' him, January neber said a word. The massa got madder and madder kaze he couldn't make January holla.

"What's the matter wid you, nigger," he say. "Don't it hurt?"

January, he neber said nothin', and the massa keep a beatin' till little streams of blood started flowin' down January's chest, but he neber holler. His lips was a quiverin' and his body was a shakin', but his mouf it neber open. And all the while I sat on my mammy's and pappy's steps a cryin'. The niggers was all gathered about and some uv them could't stand it. They hadda go inside dere cabins.

Atter while, January, he couldn't stand it no longer hisself, and he say in a hoarse loud whisper: "Massa! Massa! Have mercy on dis poor nigger."

WILLIAM COLBERT, son of Onie and Jim Colbert, was born into slavery about 1844 on a plantation owned by Jim Hodison in Fort Valley, Georgia. William Colbert left the plantation after the Civil War. He married, but his wife died about 1900. He lived alone in a cabin in Birmingham, Alabama.

My mammy she trouble in her heart bout the way they treated.

Ever night, she pray for the Lawd to git her and her chillun out ob the place. One day, she plowin' in the cotton fiel'. All sudden like she let out big yell. Then she sta't singin' and a shoutin' and a whoopin' and a hollowin'. Then it seem she plow all the harder. When she come home, Marse Jim's mammy say, "What all that goin' on in the fiel'? Yo' think we sen' you out there jes to whoop and yell? No siree, we put you out there to work and you sho' bettah work else we git the overseeah to cowhide you ole black back."

My mammy jes grin all over her black wrinkled face and say: "I's saved. The Lawd done tell me I's saved. Now I know the Lawd will show me the way. I ain't gwine a grieve no more. No matter how much yo' all done beat me and my chillun the Lawd will show me the way. And some day we nevah be slaves."

Ole Granny Moore grab the cowhide and slash mammy cross the back, but mammy nebber yell.

She jes go back to the fiel' a singin'.

FANNIE MOORE, daughter of Rachel and Stephen Andrew Moore, was born into slavery about 1849 on a plantation owned by Jim and Mary Anderson Moore in Moore, South Carolina. She was interviewed in Asheville, North Carolina, and died three years later.

One slave name Bob Love.

When massa start to whip him he cuts his throat and dives into de river.

He am dat scairt of a whippin' dat he kilt himself.

WALTER RIMM was born into slavery about 1857 on a plantation owned by Captain Hatch in San Patricio County, Texas, near Corpus Christi. There are dozens of accounts of suicides similar to Rimm's in the Slave Narratives. After freedom, Rimm helped his father on a farm, worked as a cook at the nearby King Ranch and moved to Fort Worth. He married Minnie Bennett and later Agnes Skelton, with whom he raised five children.

Marse John hab a big plantation an' lots of slaves. Dey treated us purty good, but we hab to wuk hard.

Time I was ten years ole I was makin' a reg'lar han' 'hin' de plow. Oh, yassuh, Marse John good 'nough to us an' we git plenty to eat, but he had a oberseer name Green Bush what sho' whup us iffen we don't do to suit him. Yassuh, he' mighty rough wid us, but he didn't do de whuppin' hisse'f.

He had a big black boy name Mose, mean as de debil an' strong as a ox, and de oberseer let him do all de whuppin'. An', man, he could sho' lay on dat rawhide lash. He whupped a nigger gal 'bout thirteen years ole so hard she nearly die. An' allus atterwa'ds she hab spells of fits or somp'n.

WALTER CALLOWAY was born into slavery about 1848 in Richmond, Virginia. He was forced to relocate when he was sold to John Calloway, who lived in Snowdoun, Alabama. He worked for the Birmingham street department for at least 25 years—until just a few months before his interview.

I sho' has had a ha'd life. Jes wok, and wok, and wok. I nebbah know nothin' but wok. De rich white folks nebbah did no wok; they had da'kies t' do it foah dem. In the summah, we had t' wok outdoo's, in the wintah in the house. I had t' ceard and spin till ten o'clock. Nebbah git much rest.

Had t' git up at foah the nex' mawnin' and sta't agin. Didn' get much t' eat, nuthah, jes a lil' cawn bread and 'lasses. Lawdy, honey, yo' caint know whut a time I had. All cold 'n' hungry. No'm, I aint tellin' no lies. It de gospel truf. It sho is.

No'm, I nebbah knowed whut it wah t' rest. I jes wok all the time f 'om mawnin' till late at night. I had t' do ebbathin' they wah t' do on the outside. Wok in the field, chop wood, hoe cawn, till sometime I feels lak mah back sholy break. I done ebbathin' 'cept split rails. Ole Boss he send us niggahs out in any kine ob weathah, rain o' snow, it nebbah mattah. We had t' go t' the mountings, cut wood and drag it downt' the house. Many the time we come in wif ouh cloes stuck t' ouh poah ole cold bodies, but 'twarn't no use t' try t' git them dry. Ef the Ole Boss o' the Ole Missie see us they yell: Git on out ob heah yo' black thin', and git yo' wok outen the way!

An' Lawdy, honey, we knowed t' git, else we git the lash. They did'n' cah how ole o' how young yo' wah, yo' nebbah too big t' git the lash.

Law, chile, nobuddy knows how mean da'kies wah treated.

SARAH GUDGER, daughter of Hemphill and Smart Gudger, said she was born into slavery in 1816 on a plantation owned by Andy Hemphill in North Carolina. Records, accounts by neighbors and her detailed memories seemed to back her remarkable claim. She was interviewed in Asheville and believed to be one of the oldest people in the world in 1938 when she died at the age of 122.

I been here! I seen things! I tell you. Thousand of them things happen, but I try to forget 'em.

The worst thing I members was the colored oberseer. He was the one straight from Africa. He the boss over all the mens and womens and if 'omans don't do all he say, he lay task on them they ain't able to do.

My mother won't do all he say. When he say, "You go barn and stay till I come," she ain't do dem. So he have it in for my mother and lay task on them she ain't able for do.

Then for punishment my mother is take to the barn and strapped down on thing called the pony. Hands spread like this and strapped to the floor, and all two both she feet been tie like this. And she been give twenty five to fifty lashes till the blood flow.

And my father and me stand right there and look and ain't able to lift a hand.

BEN HORRY, son of Duffine Horry, was born into slavery in 1852 on the Brookgreen Plantation owned by Joshua Moore at Murrells Inlet, South Carolina. He sold oysters and ran a small grocery store after the war. Brookgreen is now Brookgreen Gardens, a sculpture park, garden and nature preserve near the Atlantic Ocean. Horry married twice and raised five children.

I can't say Marse Garrett wa'n't good to us motherless chillun but de overseer, Mr. Woodson Tucker, was mean as anybody.

He'd whup you nigh 'bout to deaf, and had a whuppin' log what he strip 'em buck naked and lay 'em on de log. He whup 'em wid a wide strop, wider'n my han', den he pop de blisters what he raise and 'nint 'em wid red pepper, salt, and vinegar. Den he put 'em in de house dey call de pest house and have a 'oman stay dere to keep de flys offen 'em 'twell dey get able to move.

Den dey had reg'lar men in de fields wid spades, and iffen you didn't do what you git tole, de overseer would wrop dat strap 'roun' his han' and hit you in de haid wid de wooden handle 'til he kilt you. Den de mens would dig a hole wid de spades and throw 'em in hit right dere in de fiel' jes' lack dey was cows. Didn't have no funeral nor nothin'.

LAURA CLARK, daughter of Rachel Powell, was born into slavery about 1851 on a plantation owned by Pleasant Powell in North Carolina. At about age seven, she was sold to a slaveholder by the name of Garrett, who forcibly moved her to Livingston, Alabama. She never saw her mother again. Clark married Cary Crockett and raised several children. She lived in a cabin near Livingston.

My old granddad done told me all 'bout conjure and voodoo and luck charms and signs.

De old voodoo doctors was dem what had de most power, it seem, over de nigger befo' and after de war. Dey has meetin' places in secret and a voodoo kettle, and nobody know what am put in it, maybe snakes and spiders and human blood. No tellin' what.

De big, black nigger in the corn field mos' allus had three charms round he neck: to make him fort'nate in love, and to keep him well, and one for Lady Luck at dice to be with him. Den if you has indigestion, wear a penny 'round da neck.

De power of the rabbit foot am great. One nigger used it to run away with. His old granny done told him to try it and he did. He conjures hisself by takin' a good soapy bath so the dogs can't smell him. And then say a hoodoo over he rabbit foot and go to the creek and git a start by wadin'.

They didn't miss him till he clear gone, and that show what de rabbit foot done for him.

PATSY MOSES, daughter of Lucy and Preston Armstrong, was born into slavery about 1863 on a plantation owned by the Armstrong family in Fort Bend County, Texas. Enslaved men and women like Moses cherished objects as charms to promote good health, good luck and protection. She worked as a laundress in Mart, Texas, and died in 1951.

I 'member my grandma and grandpa. In dem days de horned toads runs over de world, and my grandpa would gather 'em and lay 'em in de fireplace till dey dried, and roll 'em with bottles till dey like ashes and den rub it on de shoe bottoms.

You see, when dey wants to run away, dat stuff don't stick all on de shoes. It stick to de track. Den dey carries some of dat powder and throws it as far as dey could jump, and den jump over it and do dat again till dey use all de powder.

Dat throwed de common hounds off de trail altogether. But dey have de bloodhounds, hell hounds we calls 'em, and dey could pick up dat trail.

Dey run my grandpa over 100 mile and three or four days and nights and found him under a bridge. What dey put on him was enough!

JOHN BARKER, whose parents had the surname of Goodman, was born into slavery in 1853 at a home owned by the Barker family near Cincinnati. As a child, he was forcibly moved to Missouri and Texas by his slaveholders. After freedom, Barker worked for the army and married three times. He lived with his wife in a cottage in Houston.

Some of dere slaves would run away and hide in de woods and mos' of 'em was kotched with dogs.

Fin'ly dey took to puttin' bells on de slaves so iffen dey run away, dey could hear 'em in de woods.

GEORGE SIMMONS was born into slavery about 1854 on a plantation owned by Steve Jaynes in Alabama. He was forcibly moved to Beaumont, Texas, during the Civil War. The bells he heard were attached to enslaved men and women to prevent their escape. It is estimated that as many as 100,000 people made their way to freedom during the centuries of slavery. Simmons was interviewed in Beaumont in 1937.

I seed slaves plenty times wid iron ban's 'roun' dey ankles an' a hole in de ban' an' a iron rod fasten to hit what went up de outside of dey leg to de wais' an' fasten to another iron ban' 'roun' de waist.

Dis yere was to keep 'em from bendin' dey legs an' runnin' away. Dey call hit puttin' de stiff knee on you, an' hit sho' made 'em stiff !

Sometimes hit made 'em sick, too, caze dey had dem iron ban's so tight roun' de ankles, dat when dey tuck 'em off live things was under 'em, an' dat's whut give 'em fever, dey say. . . . Miss, whar was de Lord in dem days? Whut was He doin'?

GEORGE CHAPMAN YOUNG, son of Mary Ann Chapman and Sam Young, was born into slavery in 1846 on a plantation owned by Reuben Chapman, an absentee landlord who served in the U.S. House of Representatives and as governor of Alabama. Young married a woman named Glover and worked as a farm laborer. He lived his entire life near the plantation in Livingston, Alabama, and died in 1943.

Marse Bob had some nigger dogs like other places and used to train them for fun. He'd git some the boys to run for a hour or so and then put the dogs on the trail.

Old man Briscoll, who had a place next to ours, was vicious cruel. He was mean to his own blood, beatin' his chillen. His slaves was afeared all the time and hated him.

Old Charlie—a good, old man who 'longed to him—run away and stayed six months in the woods 'fore Briscoll cotched him. The niggers used to help feed him, but one day a nigger 'trayed him, and Briscoe put the dogs on him and cotched him.

He made to Charlie like he wasn't goin' to hurt him none, and got him to come peaceful. When he took him home, he tied him and beat him for a turrible long time. Then he took a big, pine torch and let burnin' pitch drop in spots all over him.

Old Charlie was sick 'bout four months and then he died.

ANDREW GOODMAN, son of Martha and Dave Goodman, was born into slavery about 1849 on a plantation owned by Bob Goodman near Birmingham, Alabama. His mother spun wool; his father was a shoemaker. At age three, Andrew and his family were forcibly moved to Smith County, Texas. After the war, he married and raised seven children, but he lost track of them all in old age.

De pattyroller was a man who watched foh de slaves what try to run away. I see dem sneakin in an out dem bushes. When dey fine im de give im a good whippin.

JULIA WILLIAMS, whose mother was named Katharine, was born into slavery about 1840 on a plantation near Richmond, Virginia. The pattyrollers she refers to policed the South, capturing black men and women who were off their plantations without a pass. Their treatment of the enslaved was especially brutal. After the war, Julia married Richard Williams and raised eight children. She moved with him to Ohio and was a charter member of the Wadsworth Colored Baptist Church.

One day atter I finish' my chores, I slip off an' go across the line to see my mammy. When I was a-comin' back th'ough the woods, I met up wid two pattyrollers. They stop me and say, "Nigger, who you belong to?" "Massa Jim Johnson," I answers. "Whut you a doin' out here, den?" they say, all the time a slippin' a little closer so's to grab me.

I don't take time to gib them no mo' answers kaze I knowd that dis meant a beatin'. I starts my legs a-flyin' and I runs through the fores' lak a scar't rabbit wid them pattyrollers right behin' me. My bare feets flew over them stones and I jus' hit the high spots in the groun'. I knowed them two mens didn't have no chance to kotch me, but dis sho meant a whuppin' when I got home.

But I didn't go home that night. I stay out in the woods and buil' me a little fiah. I laid down under a sycamo' tree a-tryin' ter make up my min' ter go and take that beatin'. I heered the panthers a screamin' a way off in the fores' and the wildcats a howlin', and how I wished I coulda been wid my mammy.

Warn't no use of me a-cryin' kaze I was a long way fum home and dere warn't no one to could hear me.

Soon I fell slap to sleep on a bed of moss. The nex' day I was awful hongry, and long 'bout the time the sun was a-comin' ober the ridge, I heerd some mens a-comin' through the brush. It was the massa, the oberseer and some mo' mens. I runs toward the massa and I calls as loud as I could: "Massa Jim, here I is."

STEPNEY UNDERWOOD, son of Ella and Charlie Underwood, was born into slavery about 1855 on a plantation owned by the Johnson family in Alabama. His parents lived on neighboring plantations in Lowndes County. After the war, he married twice and worked as a farmer and laborer in Birmingham. He died in 1938.

Iffen a nigger run away and dey cotch him, or does he come back 'cause he hongry, I seed Uncle Jake [the overseer] stretch him out on de ground and tie he hands and feet to posts so he can't move none.

Den he git de piece of iron what he call de "slut" and what is like a block of wood with little holes in it, and fill de holes up with tallow and put dat iron in de fire till de grease sizzlin' hot and hold it over de pore nigger's back and let dat hot grease drap on he hide. Den he take de bullwhip and whip up and down. And after all dat throw de pore nigger in de stockhouse and chain him up a couple days with nothin' to eat.

My papa carry de grease scars on he back till he die.

SARAH FORD, daughter of Jane Christopher and Mike Mitchell, was born into slavery about 1854 on a plantation owned by Kit Patton in West Columbia, Texas. Her father and mother were killed in a cataclysmic windstorm in 1875 on the day Sarah gave birth to her first child. She and husband Wes Ford raised eleven children. She lived in a small cottage in East Columbia and died in 1945.

Marse Tom was a fitty man for meanness. He jus' 'bout had to beat somebody every day to satisfy his cravin'.

He had a big bullwhip and he stake a nigger on the ground and make 'nother nigger hold his head down with his mouth in the dirt and whip the nigger till the blood run out and red up the ground. We li'l niggers stand round and see it done. Then he tell us, "Run to the kitchen and git some salt from Jane." That my mammy; she was cook. He'd sprinkle salt in the cut, open places and the skin jerk and quiver and the man slobber and puke. Then his shirt stick to his back for a week or more.

Some Sundays we went to church some place. We allus liked to go any place. A white preacher allus told us to 'bey our masters and work hard and sing and when we die we go to heaven. Marse Tom didn't mind us singin' in our cabins at night, but we better not let him cotch us prayin'.

Seems like niggers jus' got to pray. Half they life am in prayin'. Some nigger take turn 'bout to watch and see if Marse Tom anyways 'bout. Then they circle theyselves on the floor in the cabin and pray. They git to moanin' low and gentle, "Some day, some day, some day, this yoke gwine be lifted offen our shoulders."

Marse Tom been dead long time now. I 'lieve he's in hell. Seem like that where he 'long.

WILLIAM MOORE, son of Jane and Ray Moore, was born into slavery about 1855 on a plantation owned by Tom Waller in Selma, Alabama. The Wallers relocated their plantation to Mexia, in eastern Texas. After the war, William, his wife and children moved to nearby Corsicana. He worked as a farmer and sheepherder. He was interviewed in Dallas.

PART IV

WAR AND FREEDOM

PLANTATION HOUSE
INHABITED BY
DESCENDANTS OF FORMER
SLAVES, NEAR RIDGE,
MARYLAND, 1941.
JOHN COLLIER PHOTO

'A deep impression'

I remember the beginning of the war well. The conditions made a deep impression on my mind, and the atmosphere of Washington was charged with excitement and expectations. There existed considerable need for assistance to the Negroes who had escaped after the war began, and Reverend Cain took a leading part in rendering aid to them.

They came into the city without clothes or money, and no idea of how to secure employment. A large number were placed on farms, some given employment as domestics and still others mustered into the federal army.

The city was one procession of men in blue, and the air was full of martial music. The fife and drum could be heard almost all the time, so you may imagine what emotions a colored person of my age would experience.

ANN J. EDWARDS was born into slavery in 1856 at a home owned by John J. Cook in Arlington County, Virginia. She and her parents were manumitted, or set free, in 1857, but her mother and father soon separated and her mother died in 1861. Ann was adopted by Richard H. Cain, an African American minister who later served in the South Carolina Senate and U.S. House. She attended Howard College (now Howard University) where she met and married James E. Edwards. They worked as ministers in Los Angeles and Kansas City. She was living with her granddaughter in Fort Worth when interviewed.

The town was filled with soldiers for several days. They assembled about the courthouse and had speakings. One day I passed there with my papa and saw Abraham Lincoln hanging from a noose in the courthouse square. Of course, it was only an effigy of Abraham Lincoln which was used to show what the soldiers thought of him.

Papa told me that the soldiers shot the effigy full of bullet holes before they left town.

ESTHER KING CASEY, born into slavery in 1856, was about five years old when her family was sold to Henry King of Americus, Georgia. After the war, King's wife paid for Esther's public schooling as long as she stayed on the plantation. Esther started teaching in public schools, but quit after she married Jim Casey. They farmed in southern Georgia and raised one child. In 1937, she was living with her grandchildren in Birmingham, Alabama.

I see lots of sojers. Dey so many like hair on your head. Dey Yankees. Dey call 'em bluejackets. Dey a fight up near massa's house.

Us climb in tree for to see. Us hear bullets go zoom through de air 'round dat tree, but us didn't know it was bullets.

A man rid up on a hoss and tell massa to git us pickaninnies out dat tree or dey git kilt.

ORELIA ALEXIE FRANKS, daughter of Fanire and Alexis Martin, was born into slavery about 1847 on a plantation owned by Valerien Martin near Opelousas, Louisiana. She and 3 million people in ten Confederate states were legally freed by President Lincoln's Emancipation Proclamation in 1863. But most did not gain freedom until 1865, when the U.S. Army controlled the South. Franks was living in Beaumont, Texas, in 1937. She died two years later.

I and my mistis and her baby hid in de swamps three days while Sherman and his army was passin' through. Marse Rogers was in Virginny, and when he got back home there wasn't nothin' left but a well. Everything had been burned up.

JOSEPHINE HILL was born into slavery about 1843 on a plantation owned by a man named Rogers in Georgia. She was referring to U.S. General William Tecumseh Sherman's March to the Sea in late 1864. After the Civil War, Rogers moved to Alabama to purchase another plantation. Josephine voluntarily moved with his family to work as a nursemaid to his children. She lived in Eufaula.

Gen'l Grierson and his men marched right through town. Mr. Lincoln done said we was free, but us lil' niggers was too skeered to lissen to any ban' music, even iffen the so'jers had come to set us free.

GUS ASKEW was born into slavery about 1853 on a plantation owned by the Edwards family in Henry County, Alabama. He was forcibly moved to Eufaula near the end of the Civil War. The raid he witnessed by U.S. Army Major General Benjamin H. Grierson was in April 1865, the last month of the Civil War. Askew later married and raised a family. He worked as a blacksmith and was interviewed in Eufaula.

I sho' was glad when freedom come, 'cause dey jus' ready to put my little three-year-old boy in de field. Dey took 'em young.

BETTY SIMMONS was born into slavery about 1836 on a plantation owned by Leftwidge Carter in Macedonia, Alabama. She was presented as a wedding gift to Carter's daughter and new son-in-law, who sold Betty to settle financial affairs. She was forcibly moved to New Orleans, where she was sold again. She married George Fortescue and raised a family. She lived in Beaumont, Texas.

Soldiers, all of a sudden, was everywhere—comin' in bunches, crossin' and walkin' and ridin'. Everyone was a-singin'. We was all walkin' on golden clouds. Hallelujah!

Everybody went wild. We all felt like heroes, and nobody had made us that way but ourselves. We was free. Just like that we was free. It didn't seem to make the whites mad, either. They went right on giving us food just the same.

Nobody took our homes away, but right off colored folks started on the move. They seemed to want to get closer to freedom, so they'd know what it was. Like it was a place or a city. Me and my father stuck—stuck close as a lean tick to a sick kitten.

We knowed freedom was on us, but we didn't know what was to come with it. We thought we was goin' to get rich like the white folks. We thought we was goin' to be richer than the white folks 'cause we was stronger and knowed how to work, and the whites didn't, and they didn't have us to work for them anymore.

FELIX HAYWOOD, son of Elsie and Tecompre Haywood, was born into slavery about 1844 on a plantation owned by William Gudlow in St. Hedwig, Texas. News of the emancipation spread slowly to Texas. It was not until June 19, 1865, two months after the end of the Civil War, when most enslaved Texans learned of their freedom. Felix was a sheepherder and cowpuncher, and worked as a laborer at the San Antonio waterworks. He died six months after his 1937 interview.

Mother was workin' in the house, and she cooked too. She say she used to hide in the chimney corner and listen to what the white folks say.

When freedom was 'clared, marster wouldn' tell 'em, but mother she hear him tellin' mistus that the slaves was free but they didn' know it, and he's not gwineter tell 'em till he makes another crop or two.

When mother hear that, she say she slip out the chimney corner and crack her heels together four times and shouts, "I's free, I's free." Then she runs to the field, 'gainst marster's will and tol' all the other slaves—and they quit work.

Then she run away and in the night she slip into a big ravine near the house, and have them bring me to her. Marster, he come out with his gun and shot at mother, but she run down the ravine and gits away with me.

TEMPIE CUMMINS, daughter of Charlotte Brooks and Jim Starkins, was born into slavery about 1863 on a plantation owned by William Neyland in Brookeland, Texas. As a baby, she was handed over to Fannie Neyland. After the war, she worked as a servant. She married Bill Cummins about 1881 and they raised ten children. She was widowed by the time she was interviewed, living alone in Jasper, Texas. She died in 1959.

When de war am over, de marster come home and he calls all us cullud folks to de house and him reads a paper and says, "All yous niggers am free, and you can go whar you wants. But I 'vises yous not to go till yous has a place for work and make de livin.'"

All de niggers stay at fust, den leave one 'fter 'nother.

TILLIE R. POWERS was born about 1860 near the Washita River in Oklahoma. Her mother was kidnapped by a band of Native Americans and she was fathered by an Indian. Not wanting Tillie to grow up in the tribe, her mother wrapped the baby in a blanket and set her beside the river. She was found by Confederate army officer Joseph Powers, who raised her on a plantation in Edgecombe County, North Carolina. Plantation owners, in desperate need of help for the 1865 planting season, offered food and shelter to the formerly enslaved. Many, like young Tillie, stayed—at least for a while. She married John Daniels and moved to Texas to farm. She was interviewed in Fort Worth.

When freedom come, the master tells his slaves and says, "What you gwine do?"

Wall, suh, not one of dem knows dat. De fact am, dey's scared dey gwine be put off de place. But master says dey can stay and work for money or share crop. He says they might be trouble 'twixt de whites and niggers, and likely it be best to stay and not git mixed in dis and dat org'ization.

JAMES W. SMITH was born into slavery about 1860 on a plantation owned by John Hallman in Palestine, Texas. Smith farmed for several decades after the war. The concept of sharecropping seemed reasonable. Landowners possessed capital, property, housing and equipment. The formerly enslaved knew how to farm and could provide labor. But sharecropping usually left African Americans as well as white laborers deep in debt and misery. Smith, who became a Baptist minister, married Jennie Goodman and lived in Fort Worth.

De end of dat war comes and old Pinchback says, "You niggers all come to de big house in de mornin.'"

He tells us we is free and he opens his book and gives us all a name and tells us whar we comes from and how old we is and says he pay us 40 cents a day to stay with him.

I stays 'bout a year and dere's no big change.

De same houses and some got whipped, but nobody got nailed to a tree by de ears like dey used to. . . . Well, time goes on some more and den Lizzie and me, we gits together and we marries reg'lar with a real weddin'.

We's been together a long time and we is happy.

JAMES GREEN, son of Delia and Isaac Green, was born into slavery in 1841 on a plantation owned by John Williams in Petersburg, Virginia. His father, an American Indian, managed to get his son declared a "free boy." But at age twelve, James was kidnapped and sold at a Virginia slave market to a Texas ranchman named James Pinchback. Green married Lizzie Robinson. After the war, he worked as a farmer in Wilson, Texas. He was living in San Antonio in 1937, and died the following year.

Well, when I is free I isn't free, 'cause de boss wants me and another boy to stay till we's 21 year old. But old Judge Longworth, he come down dere and dere was pretty near a fight, and he 'splains to us we was free.

WILLIAM GREEN was born into slavery about 1850. He was forcibly moved from Mississippi to Texas during the Civil War by slaveholder John Montgomery. Slavery officially ended with the ratification of the Thirteenth Amendment in late 1865. After the war, Green worked as a tenant farmer and preacher. He lived in San Antonio.

Massa Hall, he say we kin stay, and he pay us for the work. We didn' have nothin', so most of us stays gatherin' the crop. Some of them gits the patch of land from massa and raises a bale of cotton. Massa buy that cotton and then he sell it.

After 'while they slips away. Some of them works for the white folks and some of them goes to farmin' on what they calls the shares. I works nearly everywhere for the white folks and makes 'nough to eat and git the clothes.

It was harder 'n bein' the slave at first, but I likes it better, 'cause I kin go whar I wants and git what I wants.

HORACE OVERSTREET, son of Jennie and Josh Overstreet, was born into slavery in 1856 on a plantation owned by M.J. Hall near Marshall, Texas. He worked much of his life as a laborer and farmer, and died in Beaumont in 1937, a few months after his interview.

I hears 'bout freedom in September and they's pickin' cotton, and a white man rides up to massa's house on a big, white hoss and the houseboy tell massa a man want see him. And he hollers, "Light, stranger."

It a gov'ment man, and he have the big book and a bunch papers and say why ain't massa turn the niggers loose. Massa say he tryin' git the crop out, and he tell massa have the slaves in. Uncle Steven blows the cow horn what they use to call to eat, and all the niggers come runnin' 'cause that horn mean, "Come to the big house, quick."

That man reads the paper tellin' us we's free, but massa make us work sev'ral months after that. He say we git 20 acres land and a mule, but we didn't git it.

Lots of niggers was kilt after freedom, 'cause the slaves in Harrison County turn loose right at freedom and them in Rusk County wasn't. But they hears 'bout it and runs away to freedom in Harrison County. And they owners have 'em bushwhacked, that shot down.

You could see lots of niggers hangin' to trees in Sabine bottom right after freedom, 'cause they catch 'em swimmin' 'cross Sabine River and shoot 'em. They sho' am goin' be lots of soul cry 'gainst 'em in Judgment!

SUSAN MERRITT, daughter of Nancy and Hobb Rollins, was born into slavery about 1850 on a plantation owned by Andrew Watt in Rusk County, Texas. After freedom, she became a sharecropper with her parents in Harrison County. She married Will Merritt and raised fifteen children. She worked as a domestic and cook, and was living with her son in 1937 near Marshall, Texas. She died the following year.

PART V

THE PAIN OF
RECONSTRUCTION

'Some day, some day'

CABIN OF A FORMER SLAVE,
HARMONY COMMUNITY,
PUTNAM COUNTY, GEORGIA, 1941.
IRVING RUSINOW PHOTO

I couldn't go to school. I beg and beg, but she kep' sayin', "Some day, some day," and I ain't never sit in a school in my life.

LOU TURNER, daughter of Maria and Sam Marble, was born into slavery about 1848 on a cattle ranch owned by Richard West and Mary Guidry in Rosedale, Texas. The period known as Reconstruction at the end of the Civil War should have been a joyful time for Turner and newly freed African Americans. Instead, they faced harsh restrictions, later known as Jim Crow laws, that stripped them of their human and civil rights. In 1937, Turner was living with her daughter, Sarah, near Beaumont, Texas.

The owners didn't want the slaves to learn to read because they were afraid they would get too smart.

ELIJAH COX, son of Kizzie and Jim Cox, lived on a plantation near Hernando, Mississippi. His family escaped into the woods near Memphis, Tennessee, and made their way to freedom in Canada. He was correct about literacy. Starting in the early 1800s, Southern states passed laws that prohibited the teaching of reading and writing to enslaved people. About 10 percent of the enslaved taught themselves—often in secret.

Nawsuh, de white folks didn't teach us to read or write.

LINDY PATTON was born into slavery about 1841 on a plantation owned by Bill Patton in Knoxville, Alabama. She was too old to take advantage of public schools that were opened to African Americans in the South after the Civil War. Many blacks saw literacy and education as the path to full citizenship and a link to religion. In 1937, she was living in the Greene County Alabama Poor House.

If they happened to be a slave on the plantation that could jes' read a little print, they would get rid of him right now. He would ruin the niggers; they would get too smart.

The' was no such thing as school here for culluds in early days. The white folks we was raised up with had pretty good education. That's why I don't talk like most cullud folks.

I was about grown, and the' was an English family settled close, about half a mile, I guess. They had a little boy. His name was Arthur Ederle, and he come over and learned me how to spell "cat" and "dog" and "hen" and such like. I was right around about 20 years old.

MONROE BRACKINS, son of Nelson and Rosanna Brackins, was born into slavery about 1853 on a plantation owned by George Reedes in Monroe County, Mississippi. As a boy, he was forcibly moved to Malone, Texas, where he learned to be a cowpuncher. After the war, he bred livestock and farmed. He married Ida Bradley and raised several children. He died in 1942 in Hondo, Texas.

Course, I didn't git no schoolin'. The white folks allus said niggers don't need no larnin'.

Some niggers larnt to write their initials on the barn door with charcoal. Then they try to find out who done that—the white folks, I mean—and say they cut his fingers off iffen they jus' find out who done it.

CHARLEY MITCHELL, son of Lucy Mitchell, was born into slavery in 1852 in a home owned by Nat and Julia Terry in Lynchburg, Virginia. He stayed with the Terry family for one year after the war, then worked in a tobacco factory and as a waiter. He married Betty Taylor and raised two children. He moved to Panola County, Texas, in 1887 and farmed by the Sabine River near Marshall, Texas. He died in 1941.

Sho', I seen de Klux after de war. But I has no 'sperience wid 'em.

My uncle, he gits whipped by 'em. What for, I don' know 'zactly, but I think it was 'bout a hoss. Marster sho' rave 'bout dat, 'cause my uncle weren't to blame.

When de Klux come de no-'count nigger sho make de scatterment. Some climb up de chimney or jump out de winder and hide in de dugout and sich.

BETTY BORMER was born into slavery about 1857 on a plantation owned by M.T. Johnson in Tarrant County, Texas. After the Civil War, she moved with her parents, nine siblings and other enslaved families to property that their former slaveholder let them use until his death. She was one of many African Americans terrorized by the Ku Klux Klan, which was founded by southern whites to keep blacks in a subordinate role after the war. She married three times, raised one child and lived in Fort Worth.

Day has dances and fun till de Ku Klux org'nizes, and den it am lots of trouble. De Klux comes to de dance and picks out a nigger and whups him, jus' to keep de niggers scart. And it git so bad dey don't have no more dances or parties.

I 'members seein' Faith Baldwin and Jeb Johnson and Dan Hester gittin' whupped by de Klux. Dey wasn't so bad after women.

It am allus after dark when dey comes to de house and catches de man and whups him for nothin'. Dey has de power, and it am done for to show dey has de power. It gits so bad round dere, dat de menfolks allus eats supper befo' dark and takes a blanket and goes to de woods for to sleep. Alex Buford don't sleep in de house for one whole summer.

No one knowed when de Klux comin'. All a-sudden up dey gallops on hosses, all covered with hoods, and bust right into de house. Jus' latches 'stead of locks was used dem days. Dey comes sev'ral times to Alex' house, but never cotches him. I'd hear dem comin' when dey hit de lane and I'd holler, "De Klux am comin'."

WILLIAM HAMILTON was left behind on a plantation owned by Alex Buford during the war. A slave trader traveling past Buford's property in eastern Texas told the owner he would return to pick up the boy after selling his parents and other enslaved people—but the trader never came back. Hamilton, who did not know his age, was raised by the Buford family. He worked as a sharecropper after the war, married Effie Coleman, but was a widower when interviewed in a Fort Worth shack.

Arter we was mahied and was gittin' use to bein' free niggahs and happy in our cabin, one night a gen'ulman from the no'th was to see us and he tol' us if we'd go wid him he'd pay us big wages and gin us a fine house to boot.

We lef' ev'y thing there 'ceptin' whut we tied up in a bandana han'chief, and we tied that onto a stick, for the gen'ulman from the no'th wouldn't let us take no baggage.

Li'l missy, when we got dar whar he was a-takin' us, we foun' the big wages to be fifty cents a month. And that fine house tu'ned out to be mo' like a stable. Instid of our cabin and gyarden and chickens and our trees, we had a turrible place, right out under the hot sun wid watah miles away down a hill.

We was a-sittin' there befo' the fire, me and my ol' woman, when we heard a stompin' like a million horses had stopped outside the do'. We tipped to the do' and peeked out an', li'l missy, whut we seed was so terrible our eyes jes' mos' popped out our haid. Dere was a million hosses all kivered in white, wid they eyes pokin' out. And a-settin' on the hosses was men kivered in white, too, tall as giants, and they eyes was a-pokin'out, too. Dere was a leader and he heldt a bu'nin' cross in his hand.

De fust thing we knowed, them Ku Kluxes had the gen'man from the no'th out of his hidin' place 'hind our house and a-settin' on one of them hosses. They nebber spoke wid him. They jes' tuk him off somewhar. We nebber knowed whar, but he di'n't come back no mo'.

GABE HINES, son of Hetty and Gabe Hines, was born into slavery about 1843 on a plantation owned by Mary and William Shipp in Cusseta, Georgia. He married Anna Hines and worked as a laborer for the City of Eufaula in Alabama. The northerner that Hines refers to may have been an agent of the Freedmen's Bureau. The bureau was established by Congress in 1865 to assist formerly enslaved people. Its effectiveness was severely hampered by the Ku Klux Klan.

After de war, de Ku Klux am org'nize and dey makes de niggers plenty trouble. Sometimes de niggers has it comin' to 'em and lots of times dey am 'posed on.

Dere a old, cullud man name George, and he don't trouble nobody. But one night de white caps—dat what dey called—comes to George's place. Now, George know of some folks what am whupped for no cause, so he prepare for dem white caps. When dey gits to he house, George am in de loft. He tell dem he done nothin' wrong and for dem to go 'way or he kill dem.

Dey say he gwine have a free sample of what he git if he do wrong, and one dem white caps starts up de ladder to git George, and George shoot him dead. 'Nother white cap starts shootin' through de ceilin'. He can't see George, but through de cracks George can see, and he shoots de second feller.

CHARLES HURT, son of Harriet and Crawford Hurt, was born into slavery about 1852 on a plantation owned by John Hurt in Oglethorpe County, Georgia. He remained at the plantation for five years after the war. He later worked as a blacksmith, carpenter and as a railroad laborer. He married twice and raised three children. He was living in Fort Worth and died in 1942.

I remembers one night raght atter the war when the Re'struction was a-goin' on. Dere was some niggers not far fum our place that said they was agoin' to take some lan' that warn't deres. Dere massa had been kilt in the war and warn't nobody 'ceptin' the mistis and some chilluns.

Well, honey, them niggers, mo' dan one hundred of 'em, commenced a riot and was a-takin' things that don't belong to 'em. That night, the white lady she come ober to our place wid a wild look on her face. She tell Massa Bennett whut them niggers is up to and widout sayin' a word, Massa Bennett putt his hat on an lef' out the do'.

Twarn't long atter that when some hosses was heered down the road, and I look out my cabin window which was raght by the road, and I saw acomin' up through the trees a whole pack of ghosties. I thought they was, anyways. They was all dressed in white, and dere hosses was white, and they galloped faster dan the win' raght past my cabin. Then I heered a nigger say: "De Ku Klux is atter somebody."

Dem Ku Klux went ober to that lady's plantation and told them niggers that iffen they ever heered of them startin' anything mo' that they was a-goin' to tie 'em all to trees in the fores' till they all died f'um being hongry.

Atter that, dese niggers all 'roun' Louisville they kept mighty quiet.

HANNAH IRWIN, whose parents were named Hester and Sam, was born into slavery about 1857 on a plantation owned by Ryan Bennett near Louisville, Alabama. She was interviewed in nearby Eufaula.

I gits into a picklement once years ago. I's 'rested on de street. I's not done a thing, jus' walkin' 'long de street with 'nother fellow and dey claim he stole somethin'. I didn't know nothin' 'bout since.

Did dey turn me a-loose? Dey turn me loose after six months on de chain gang. I works on de road three months with a ball and chain on de legs.

ZEK BROWN was born into slavery about 1857 on a plantation owned by Green Brown in Warren County, Tennessee. Zek Brown was one of many brutalized by black codes—laws and customs in the South that prohibited African Americans from serving on juries, banned them from marrying whites and stopped them from voting. The codes also made it possible to easily arrest African Americans when they were not working. These vagrancy laws were part of a systematic strategy to provide cheap labor for white institutions. After the war, Brown married and farmed most of his life near Fort Worth.

PART VI

ONCE A SLAVE

CONFEDERATE MONUMENT IN FRONT OF THE
STATE CAPITOL, MONTGOMERY, ALABAMA, 1943.
JOHN VACHON PHOTO

'One has
his miseries'

I don't know whether it's been better since the war. At all times one has his miseries. We managed to get along on the farm. But now I have nothing.

Oh, I don't mean slavery was better than to be free. I mean times were better.

DONAVILLE BROUSSARD, son of Armance Caramouche and Neville Broussard, was born into slavery in 1850 in Lafayette, Louisiana. After the war, he managed to buy land, but like so many others he lived in the ominous shadow of the Ku Klux Klan and white hostility. The years after Reconstruction have been described as the "nadir of race relations," a period of sustained terror against African Americans, particularly in the South. Blacks were subject to arrest, rape, murder and dispossession at any time. Broussard, who moved to Beaumont, Texas, married a woman named Ordalie and raised a family. He died in 1940.

I likes to be free, but I wasn't used to it and it was hard to know how to do.

ISSABELLA BOYD was born in 1845, enslaved by Gus Wood in Richmond, Virginia. She was transported by boat—not unusual during the westward expansion of slavery before the Civil War—to Texas. After freedom, she worked as a cook on the plantation and was paid $5 a month. She left, married and raised twelve children. She worked as a laundress in Beaumont, Texas, and died soon after her interview in 1937.

They is plenty niggers in Louisiana that is still slaves. A spell back, I made a trip to where I was raised to see my old missy 'fore she died, and there was niggers in twelve or fourteen miles of that place that they didn't know they is free.

They is plenty niggers round here what is same as slaves, and has worked for white folks twenty and twenty-five years and ain't drawed a 5-cent piece. Jus' old clothes and somethin' to eat. That's the way we was in slavery.

WILLIS WINN, son of Daniel and Patsy Winn, was born well before the Civil War on a plantation owned by Bob Winn in Louisiana. He moved after the war in search of opportunity: first to Hope, Arkansas, to farm; next to Texarkana, Texas, to work in a sawmill; and then to nearby Marshall, where he lived in a one-room log cabin. He married and raised eighteen children. He was photographed holding the bugle used to wake him at four every morning before freedom.

I 'members all 'bout dem times an' de Lord know dey was better times den we got now, for white or black.

Nobody was hongry den, massa, and peoples didn't git in de devilment dey gits in now.

THEODORE FONTAINE STEWART, son of Sarah and Ed Stewart, was born about 1847 on a plantation owned by Theodore Fontaine near Florence, Georgia. He and wife Lottie raised four children. He was living in a one-room house in Eufaula, Alabama, when interviewed.

What I likes bes'—to be slave or free?

Well, it's dis way: In slavery I owns nothin' and never owns nothin'. In freedom I's own de home and raise de family.

All dat cause me worryment, and in slavery I has no worryment.

But I takes de freedom.

MARGRETT NILLIN was born into slavery about 1847 on a farm owned by Charles Corneallus in Palestine, Texas. Her father was sold just before her birth. After the war, she and her mother sewed to make a living. She married Ben Nillin and raised at least one child, whom she was living with in Fort Worth at age ninety.

I tells you 'bout de visit back to de old plantation.

I been gone near forty year and I 'cides to go back, so I reaches de house and dere am Missy Mary peelin' apples on de back gallery. She looks at me, and sh' say, "I got whippin' waiting for yous, 'cause you run off without tellin' us."

Dere wasn't no more peelin' dat day, 'cause we sits and talks 'bout de old times and de old massa. Dere sho' am de tears in dis nigger's eyes.

ALBERT HILL, whose father was named Dillion, was born into slavery about 1856 on a plantation owned by Carter Hill in Walton County, Georgia. During the war, Albert secretly carried love letters between Carter's daughter Mary and her boyfriend Bud Jackson, who fought for the Confederates and returned to marry Mary. After the war, Hill left the plantation and moved to Robinson County, Texas, where he worked on ranches and as a railroad freight handler. He was interviewed in Fort Worth.

I heared some slaves say they white folks was good to 'em, but it was a tight fight where us was.

I's thought over the case a thousand times and figured it was 'cause all men ain't made alike. Some are bad and some are good. It's like that now. Some folks you works for got no heart and some treat you white. I guess it allus will be that way.

Every nation has a flag but the cullud race.

The flag is what protects 'em. We wasn't invited here, but was brought here, and don't have no place else to go.

JORDON SMITH, whose mother was named Aggie, was born into slavery about 1851 on a Georgia plantation owned by a woman named Hicks. Upon her death, he and his mother were bequeathed to her nephew, Ab Smith, who forcibly moved them to Anderson County, Texas. After freedom, Jordon Smith worked on a steamboat crew, for a railroad and as a farmer. He was still doing odd jobs at age 86 around Marshall when he was interviewed.

My mind don't dwell back. The older I gits the lessen I thinks 'bout the old times.

MARY KINDRED, daughter of Hannah and Ruffin Hadnot, was born into slavery about 1857 on a plantation owned by Matilda and Luke Hadnot in Jasper, Texas. For people like Kindred, reflecting on the past was painful. Torture, dislocation, extreme overwork, severe abuse, inadequate nutrition, constant stress and a multitude of other trauma produced serious psychological and physical scars. Kindred raised twelve children and lived in Beaumont.

WHEN THE SLAVE
NARRATIVE PROJECT
ENDED ABOUT 1938,
MORE THAN 3,000
FORMER SLAVES HAD
BEEN INTERVIEWED
AND MORE THAN
300 HAD BEEN
PHOTOGRAPHED.

DESCENDANTS OF FORMER SLAVES,
GEE'S BEND, ALABAMA, 1937.
ARTHUR ROTHSTEIN PHOTO

WITHIN A FEW
YEARS, MANY OF THE
FORMERLY ENSLAVED
HAD DIED.

BUT THEIR WORDS
AND PICTURES
LIVE ON.

ARTELIA BENDOLPH IN HER GRANDPARENTS'
LOG HOUSE, GEE'S BEND, ALABAMA, 1937.
ARTHUR ROTHSTEIN PHOTO

GLOSSARY

afeared afraid
ah I
allus always
anudder another
atter after

bawn born
bettah better
bile boil
brudder brother
brung brought

cah care
caint can't
cawn corn
ceard card
chile child
chillen, **chillens**, **chillum** children
'clared declared
cloes clothes
cotch catch
cullud colored

dan than
dar there
dat that
de the
debil devil
dem them
dere their, there
dey they
dis this
disaway this away

ebbathin' everything
et ate

fiah fire
fine find
flo' floor
foah four
foah, **foh** for
'fore before
forgit forget
fum from
fur far
fust first

gib give
git, **gits** get
gwine going
gwineter going to
gyarden garden

hab have
haid head
hawg hog
heared, **heered** heard
helt held
hisse'f himself
holla holler
hongry hungry
hosses horses
hunnert hundred

I's I, I was, I have
iffen if
im them
instid instead

jes', **jest** just

kaze because
keeps kept
kilt killed
kin can
kivered covered
kotch catch
kotched caught

lack, **lak** like
'lasses molasses
lawd lord
'lect, 'lects recollects
lemme let me
lissen listen

mah'ied, **mahied** married
mahs, **mahster**, **marse**, **marster**, **massa** master, Mr.
mah my
missus, **missy**, **mistus** mistress, Mrs.
mistises girls
mouf mouth

nawsuh no sir
nebbah, **nebber**, **neber**, **nevah** never
neithah, **nuthah** neither
nobuddy nobody
nuss nurse

ob of
ober, **ouah** over
ole old
'omans women
ouah our
overseeah overseer
ownah owner

poah, **pore** poor
putt put

raght right

saw seen
scairt, **scar't**, **scart**, **skeered** scared
sech, **sich** such
seed saw
sho' sure
sholy surely
so'jers, **sojers** soldiers
sole sold
somepin', **somp'n** something
stays stayed
strop strap
suh sir
summah summer

ter to
'ticular particular
tole told
took taken
truf truth
turrible terrible
'twell till
'twixt between
usta used to
uv of

wah were
wall well
warn't weren't
was were
watah water
wha was
whar where
whup whip
whut what
wid with
widout without
winder window
wintah winter
wok, **wuk** work
wored wore
wrop wrap
wuzn' wasn't
wy why

yas yes
yassuh yes sir

NARRATIVES INDEX AND PHOTO CREDITS

Credits refer to the government employees who conducted the interviews and took photographs.

BIBLIOGRAPHY

Ardoin, Bobby. "Historical Marker Placed at Site of Little Known Civil War Battle near Opelousas." *Acadiana Advocate,* June 24, 2015.

Bailey, Guy, Natalie Maynor, and Patricia Cukor-Avila. *The Emergence of Black English: Text and Commentary.* John Benjamins, 1991.

Berlin, Ira, Marc Favreau, and Steven F. Miller. *Remembering Slavery: African Americans Talk about Their Personal Experiences of Slavery and Freedom.* New Press, 1998.

Bimm, Mike. "Grierson's Alabama Raid of April, 1865." *Encyclopedia of Alabama,* 25 Aug. 2015, www.encyclopediaofalabama.org/article/h-3701.

"Born in Slavery: Slave Narratives from the Federal Writers' Project, 1936 to 1938." *The Library of Congress,* www.loc.gov/collections/slave-narratives-from-the-federal-writers-project-1936-to-1938/.

Botkin, Benjamin Albert. *Lay My Burden Down: A Folk History of Slavery.* Delta, 2016.

Crew, Spencer, Lonnie Bunch, and Clement Price. *Slave Culture: A Documentary Collection of the Slave Narratives from the Federal Writers' Project.* Greenwood, 2014.

Davis, David Brion. *Inhuman Bondage: The Rise and Fall of Slavery in the New World.* Oxford University, 2008.

Davis, David Brion. *The Problem of Slavery in the Age of Emancipation.* Vintage Books, 2015.

Douglass, Frederick. *Narrative of the Life of Frederick Douglass an American Slave Written by Himself.* Race Point Publishing, 2017.

Eaves, Shannon Camille. "Navigating the Sad Epoch: Sexual Exploitation within Enslaved Communities in the Antebellum South." *University of North Carolina at Chapel Hill,* 2010.

Egypt, Ophelia Settle. *Unwritten History of Slavery: Autobiographical Accounts of Negro Ex-Slaves.* Social Science Institute, Fisk University, 1945.

Escott, Paul D. *Slavery Remembered: A Record of Twentieth-Century Slave Narratives.* University of North Carolina, 1979.

Fogel, Robert William, and Stanley L. Engerman. *Without Consent or Contract: The Rise and Fall of American Slavery.* Norton, 1994.

Franklin, John Hope, and Alfred A. Moss Jr. *From Slavery to Freedom: A History of African Americans.* Knopf, 2004.

"Fugitive Slaves in the United States." Wikipedia, Wikimedia Foundation, en.wikipedia.org/wiki/Fugitive_slaves_in_the_United_States.

Gabbin, Joanne V. *Sterling A. Brown: Building the Black Aesthetic Tradition.* Greenwood, 1985.

Garner, Lori Ann. "Representations of Speech in the WPA Slave Narratives of Florida and the Writings of Zora Neale Hurston." *Western Folklore,* vol. 59, no. 3/4, 2000, pp. 215-231.

Gates, Henry Louis Jr., and J.A. Rogers. *100 Amazing Facts about the Negro.* Pantheon Books, 2017.

Genovese, Eugene D. *Roll, Jordan, Roll: The World the Slaves Made.* Vintage Books, 1976.

Gronniosaw, James Albert Ukawsaw. *A Narrative of the Most Remarkable Particulars in the Life of James Albert Ukawsaw Gronniosaw, an African Prince, as Related by Himself.* Gale Eighteenth Century Collections Online, Print Editions, 2018.

Halpern, Rick, and Enrico Dal Lago. *Slavery and Emancipation.* Blackwell, 2002.

Hurston, Zora Neale, and Deborah G. Plant. *Barracoon: The Story of the Last "Black Cargo."* Amistad, 2018.

Jacobs, Donald M. *Index to The American Slave.* Greenwood, 1981.

Joyner, Charles. *Drums and Shadows: Survival Studies among the Georgia Coastal Negroes.* University of Georgia, 1986.

Katz-Hyman, Martha B., and Kym S. Rice. *World of a Slave: Encyclopedia of the Material Life of Slaves in the United States.* Greenwood, 2011.

Kneeland, Linda Kay. "African American Suffering and Suicide Under Slavery." *Montana State University,* 2006.

Library of Congress Abraham Lincoln Papers. Series 1. General Correspondence. 1833-1916: Edmund James McGarn and William Fairchild to Abraham Lincoln, Saturday, April 20, 1861.

Mazzari, Louis. "Arthur Raper and Documentary Realism in Greene County, Georgia." *Georgia Historical Quarterly,* vol. 87, no. 3/4, 2003, pp. 389–407.

Mormino, Gary R. "Florida Slave Narratives." *Florida Historical Quarterly,* vol. 66, no. 4, April 1988, pp. 399-419.

Perdue, Charles L., Thomas E. Barden, and Robert K. Phillips. *Weevils in the Wheat Interviews with Virginia Ex-Slaves.* University of Virginia, 1997.

Phillips, Ulrich B. *American Negro Slavery: A Survey of the Supply, Employment and Control of Negro Labor as Determined by the Plantation Regime.* Louisiana State University, 1990.

Potts, Howard E. *A Comprehensive Name Index for the American Slave.* Greenwood, 1997.

Rae, Noel. *The Great Stain: Witnessing American Slavery.* Overlook, 2018.

Rael, Patrick. *Eighty-Eight Years: The Long Death of Slavery in the United States, 1777-1865.* University of Georgia, 2015.

Rawick, George P. *From Sundown to Sunup: The Making of the Black Community.* Greenwood, 1972.

Rawick, George P. *The American Slave: A Composite Autobiography.* Greenwood, 1972-1978. Rawick, George P., editor. *The American Slave: A Composite Autobiography.* Supplement, Series 2. Greenwood, 1979.

Rawick, George P., Jan Hillegas, and Ken Lawrence, editors. *The American Slave: A Composite Autobiography.* Supplement, Series 1. Greenwood, 1977.

Rodriguez, Junius P. *Slavery in the United States: A Social, Political, and Historical Encyclopedia.* ABC-CLIO, 2007.

Rose, Willie Lee. *A Documentary History of Slavery in North America.* University of Georgia, 1999.

Sellin, Thorsten. *Slavery and the Penal System.* Quid Pro Books, 2016.

Smith, Ryan P. "How Native American Slaveholders Complicate the Trail of Tears Narrative." *Smithsonian.com,* Smithsonian Institution, 6 Mar. 2018, www.smithsonianmag.com/smithsonian-institution/how-native-american-slaveholders-complicate-trail-tears-narrative-180968339/.

Smithers, Gregory D. *Slave Breeding: Sex, Violence, and Memory in African American History.* University of Florida, 2013.

Snyder, Terri L. "Suicide, Slavery, and Memory in North America." *Journal of American History,* vol. 97, no. 1, June 2010, pp. 39-62.

Stevenson, Louise L. "The New Woman, Social Science, and the Harlem Renaissance: Ophelia Settle Egypt as Black Professional." *Journal of Southern History,* vol. 77, no. 3, August 2011, pp. 555–594.

Stewart, Catherine A. *Long Past Slavery: Representing Race in the Federal Writers' Project.* University of North Carolina, 2016. Turner, Nat, and Thomas R. Gray. *The Confessions of Nat Turner.* Classic Americana, 2000.

Tyler, Ronnie C., and Lawrence R. Murphy. *The Slave Narratives of Texas.* State House and McMurry University, 2006.

U.S., Interviews with Former Slaves, 1936-1938, www.ancestry.com/search/collections/slaveryhistoryus/.

Virginia Writers' Project. *The Negro in Virginia.* J.F. Blair, 1994.

Wiggins, David K. "The Play of Slave Children in the Plantation Communities of the Old South, 1820-1860." *Journal of Sport History,* vol. 7, no. 2, Summer 1980, pp. 21-39.

Willis, Deborah, and Barbara Krauthamer. *Envisioning Emancipation: Black Americans and the End of Slavery.* Temple University, 2017.

Yetman, Norman R. "The Background of the Slave Narrative Collection." *American Quarterly,* vol. 19, no. 3, Autumn 1967, p. 534-553.

Yetman, Norman R. *Voices from Slavery.* Holt, Rinehart and Winston, 1972.

ACKNOWLEDGMENTS

This book took more than a century to create.

The testimony from the enslaved men and woman is based on their experiences that date back to the Civil War. Each spoke with a clear voice in the 1930s, and those voices ring louder than ever. We thank John Lomax, Sterling A. Brown and other members of the Federal Writers' Project who understood the importance of gathering these words and pictures. And we thank George P. Rawick, who spent his life preserving these words.

Many people helped make this book happen. Assisting us in finding and refining a vision were librarian Lesley Williams, journalist Alex Kotlowitz, photographer Stephen Marc and historian Catherine Stewart.

Helping us better understand the actual words recorded in the Slave Narrative Collection were language specialist Richard E. McDorman and author Miles Harvey.

Encouraging us were Ronald W. Bailey, Beverly Brannan, Lonnie Bunch, R. Alden Feldon, Cheryl Finley, Bernard Friedman, Abby Ginsberg, Malika Graham-Bailey, Mark Hillesheim, Claire Holloway, Mark Jacob, Verzell James, Cindy Jones, Gail Leondar-Wright, Jonathan Logan, James McDonough, Joyce Morishita, Bert Phillips, Daniel Stamper, Bryan Stevenson, John Russick, Eric Taylor, Mark Suchomel, Jeffrey Tegge, Dan Verdick, Deborah Willis and Susanne Zuerbig.

Supporting our research were the Northwestern University Library in Evanston, Schomburg Center for Research in Black Culture in New York City as well as the Evanston and Skokie public libraries.

We were also supported by a generous grant from the Jonathan Logan Family Foundation, which has provided essential backing to our work for years.

The Library of Congress Slave Narrative Collection includes photographs of about 325 former slaves. During the course of our work, we figured that photographs of other former slaves also existed in state archives—along with written narratives. We did find about a dozen new photographs, but ended up only using photos from the D.C. collection. We were helped in our search by Shelby Beatty of the Ohio History Connection, Debbie Pendleton of the Alabama Department of Archives and History, Angela Proctor of the John B. Cade Library at Southern University and A&M College, Emily Scott of the Houston Metropolitan Research Center and Dennis Vetrovec from Indiana State Library.

Adam Green trusted us, and connected this work to today.

Caleb Burroughs oversaw editing of this book.

The most significant contributors were members of our families, who believe and support our work. They are Karen Burke, and Caedan and Christopher Jinks; Cate and Glenn Cahan; Elie, Caleb, Maddie and Millie Burroughs; Claire Cahan, Schuyler and Evergreen Cahan Smith; Aaron, Valerie and Peter Cahan.

Eighty years ago, folklorist John Lomax had a dream. He wanted the Slave Narrative Collection to read conversationally—as if former slaves had gathered at a meeting to share their experiences.

Here is a version of what that conversation might have sounded and looked like.

Richard Cahan and Michael Williams are photo historians who tell stories based on major photo collections. They are the authors of more than a dozen books, including *Un-American: The Incarceration of Japanese Americans during World War II* and *Aftershock: The Human Toll of War.* Their work can be seen at cityfilespress.com.